ADVANCED GEOMETRY BOOKS FOR KIDS

THE PYTHAGOREAN THEOREM | CHILDREN'S MATH BOOKS

BABY PROFESSOR

EDUCATION KIDS

Learning Pythagorean Theorem the easy way with different exercises. This workbook will make you love math, even more.

Have Fun Learning Kid!

SET 1

**Find the length of the third side
of each triangle**

Name:

Date:

Score:

1.

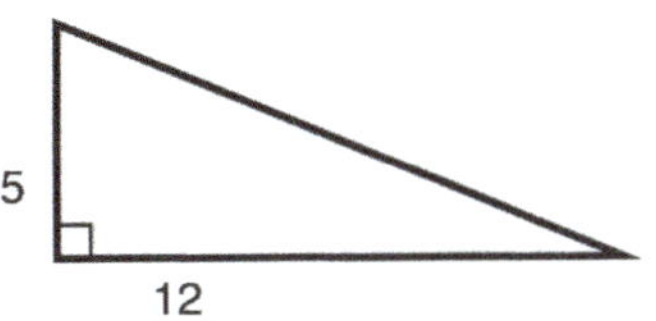

2.

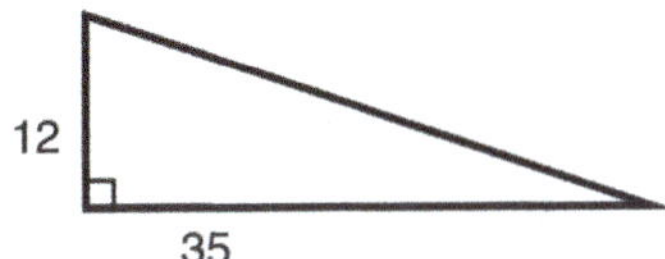

3.

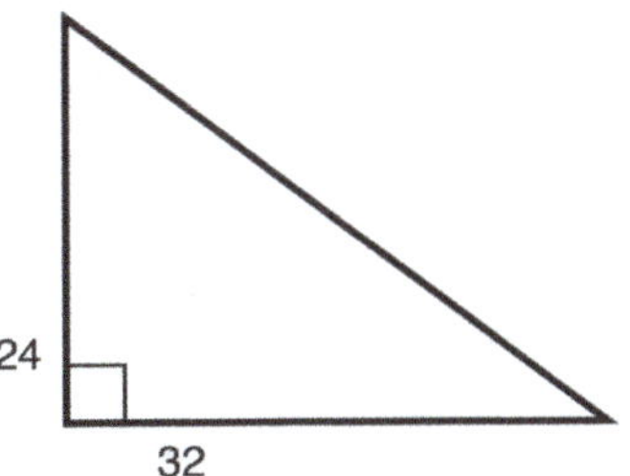

4.

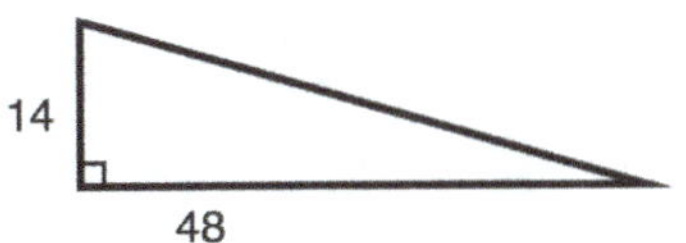

Name:

Date: ___________________ Score: ___________

1. 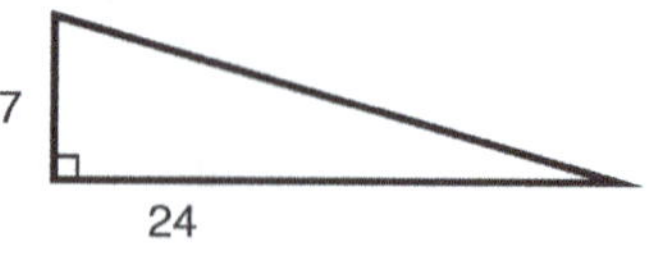

2. 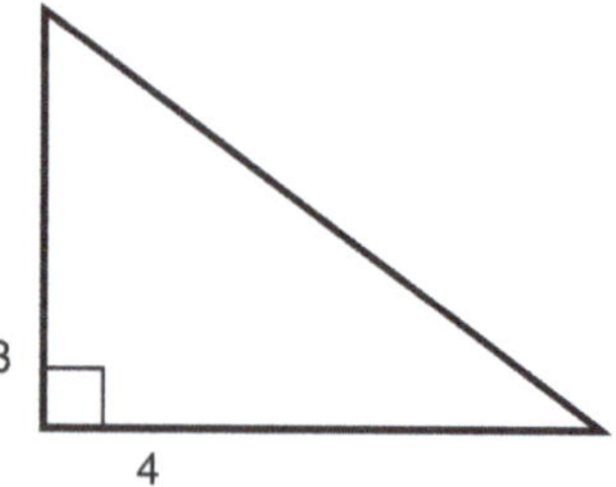

3. 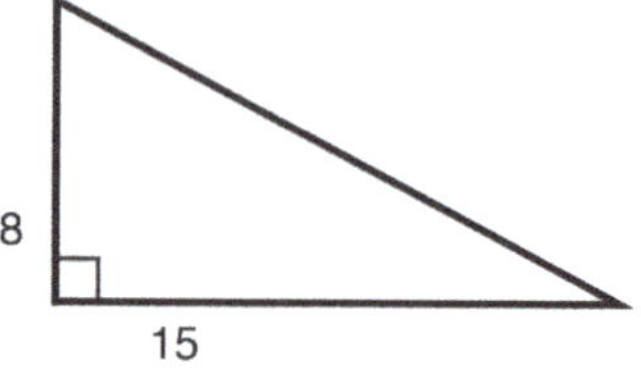

4. 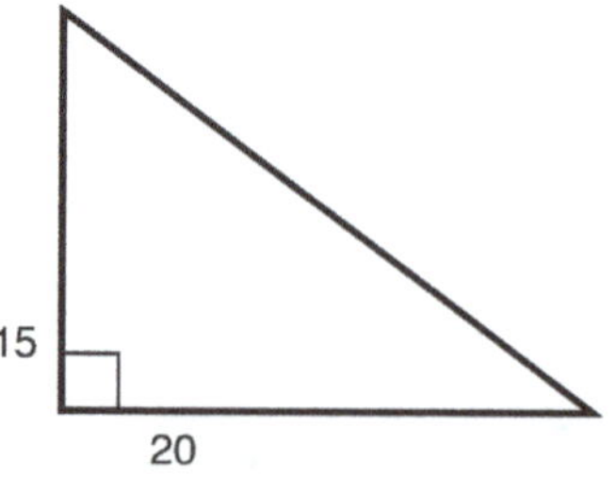

Name:

Date:

Score:

1. 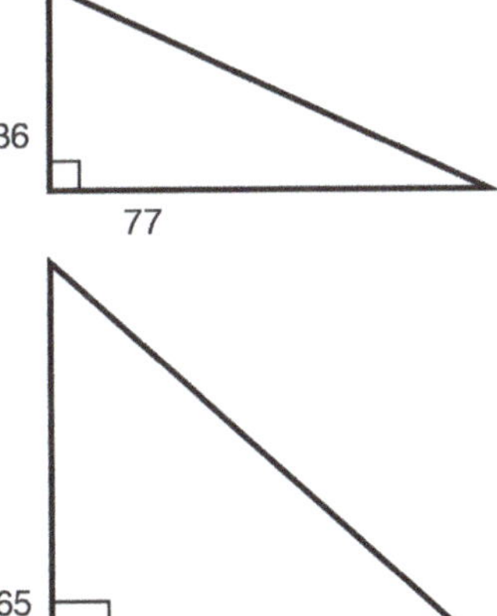

2.

3. 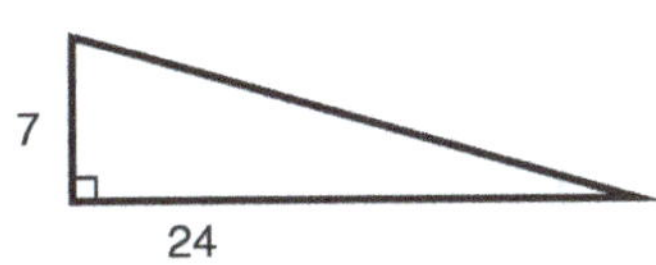

4. 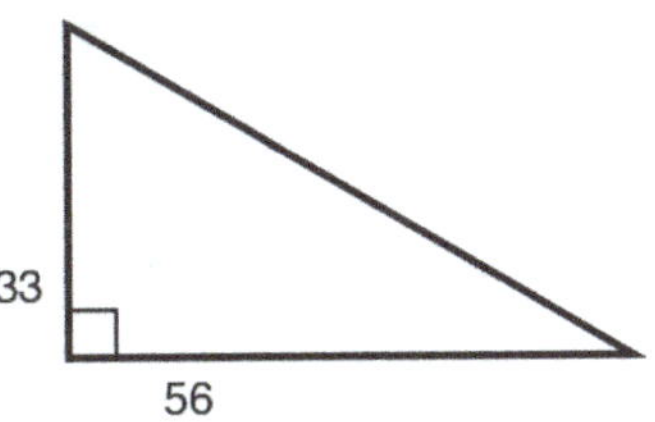

Name: _____________________________

Date: _____________________ Score: _____________

1. 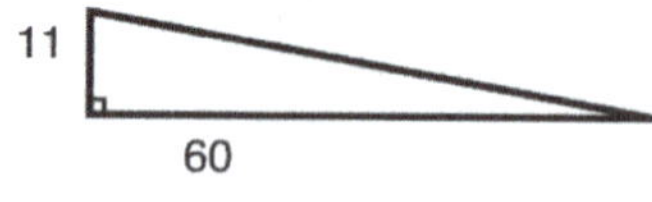

2. 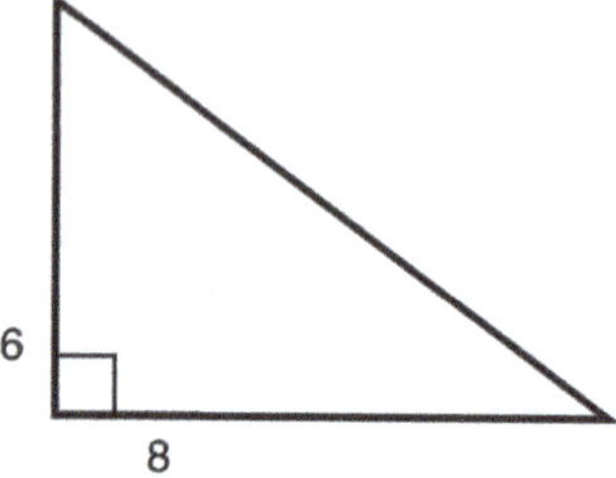

3. 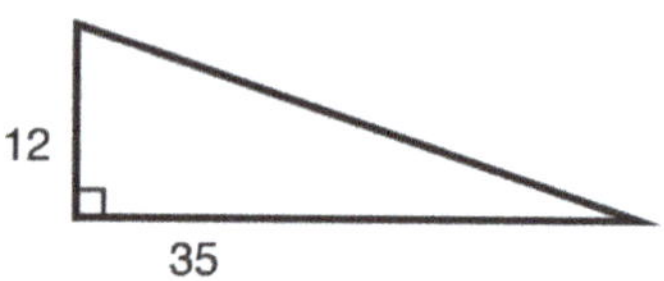

4. 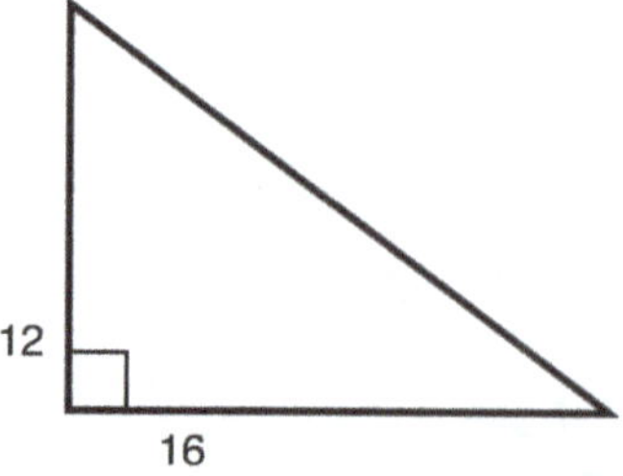

Name:

Date: Score:

1.
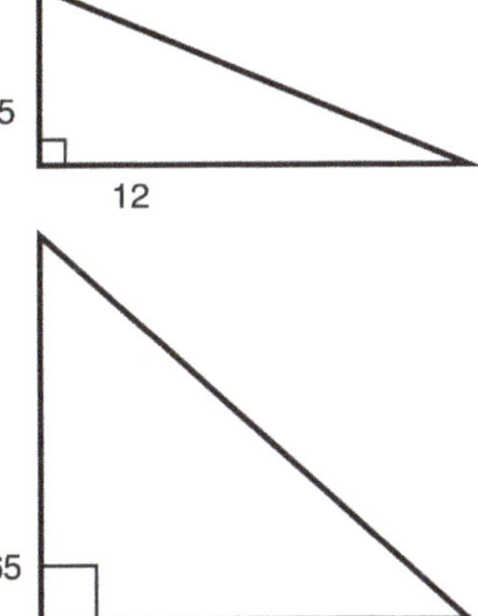

2.

3.

4.
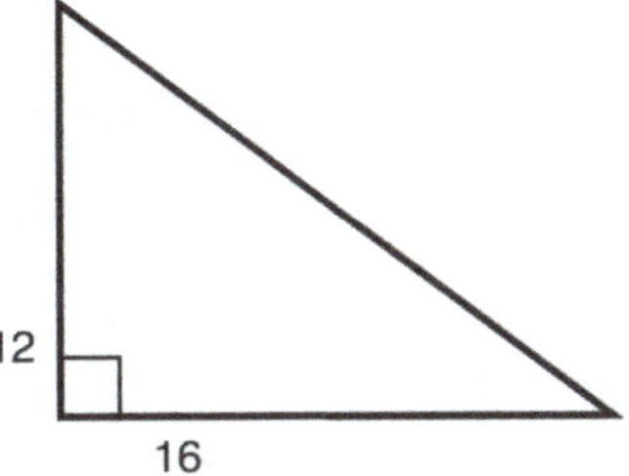

Name:

Date: Score:

1.

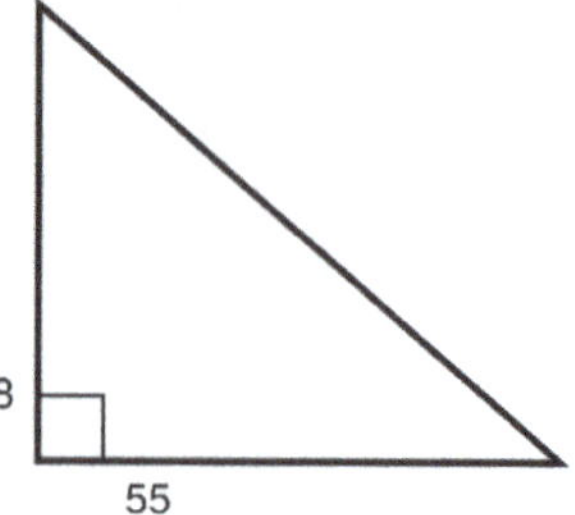

2.

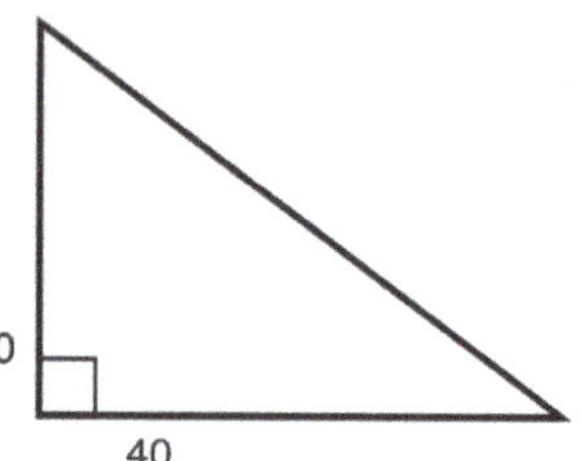

3.

4.

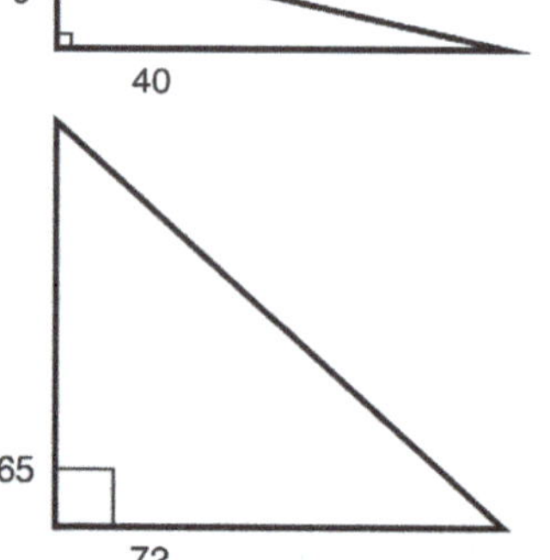

Name:

Date:

Score:

1.

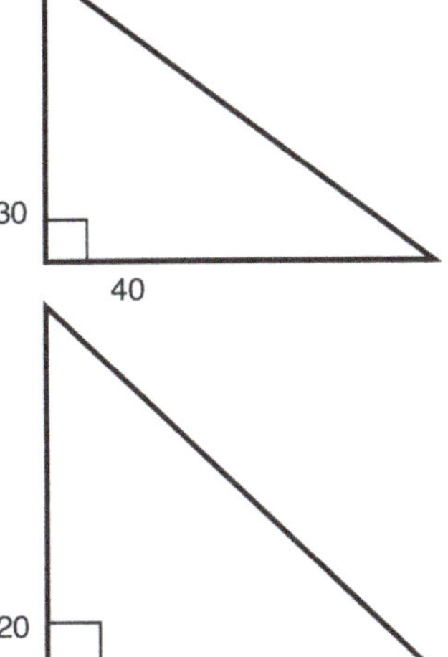

2.

3.

4.

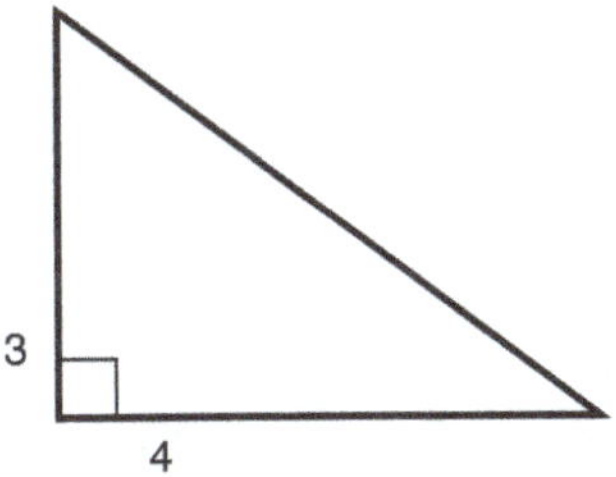

Name: ....

Date: .... Score: ....

1.

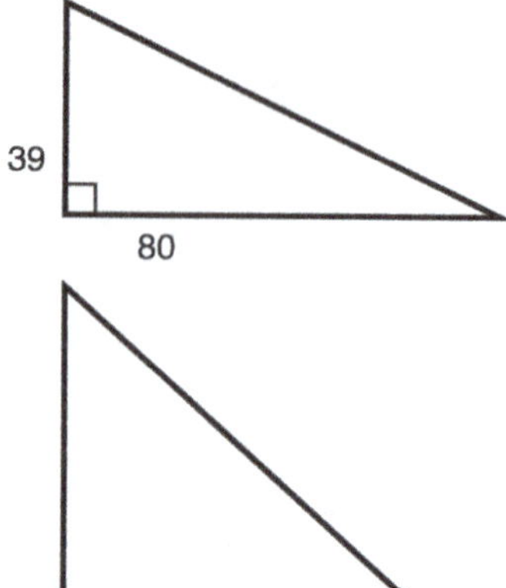

2.

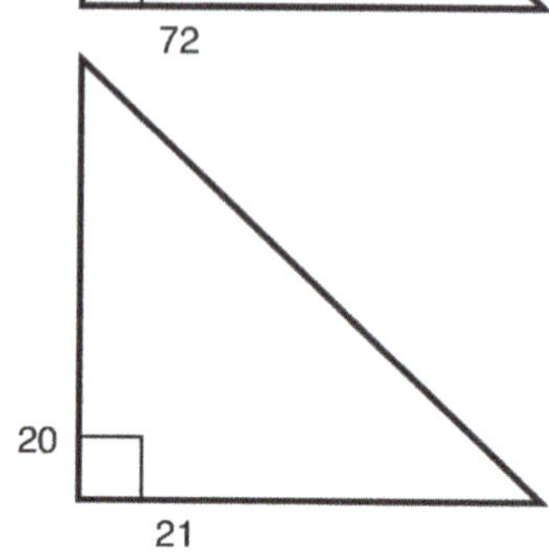

3.

4.

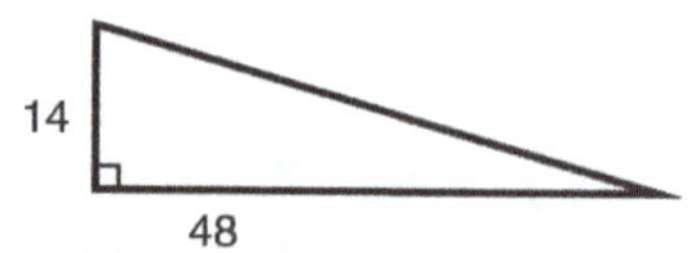

Name:

Date: Score:

1.
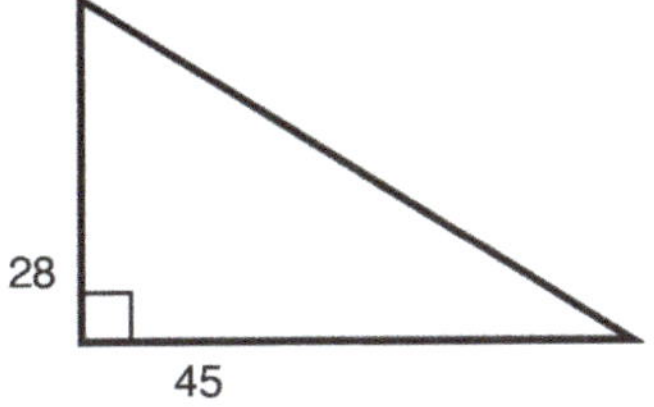

2.
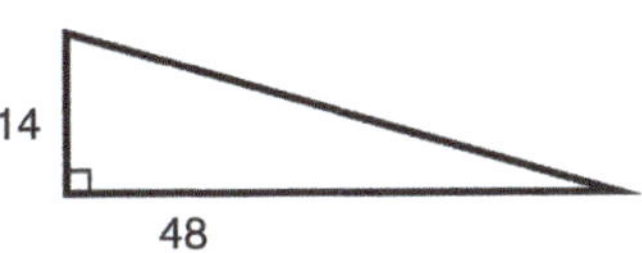

3.
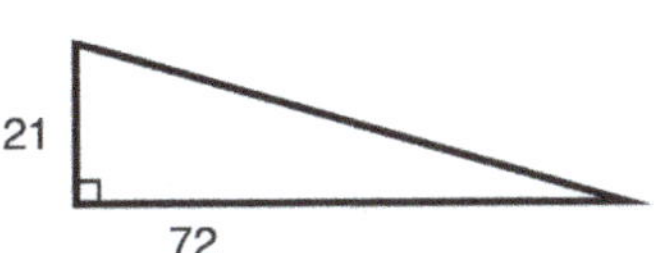

4.
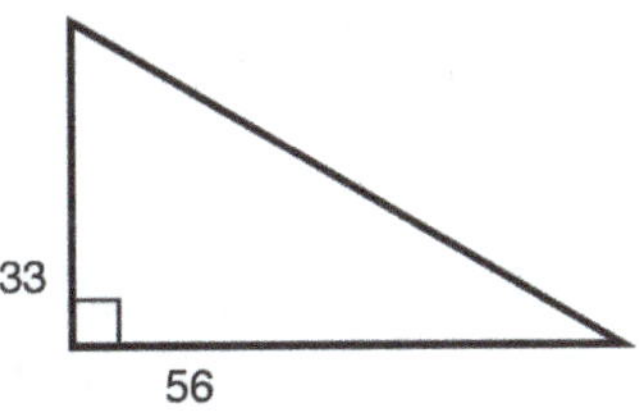

Name:

Date: Score:

1.

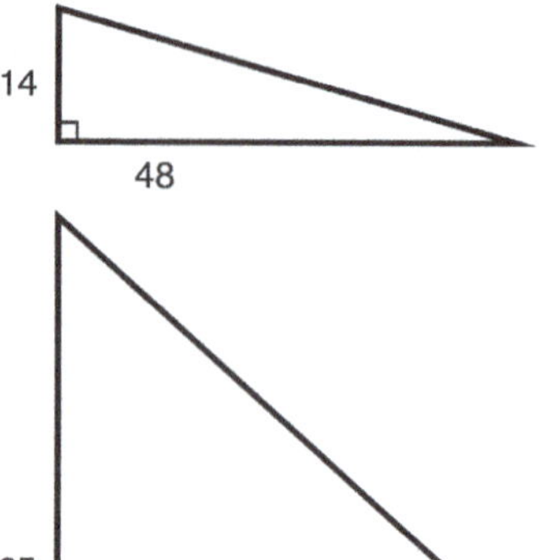

2.

3.

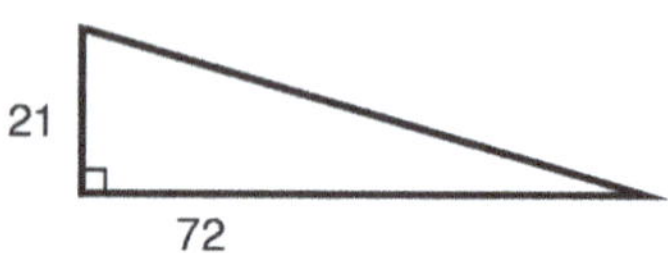

4.

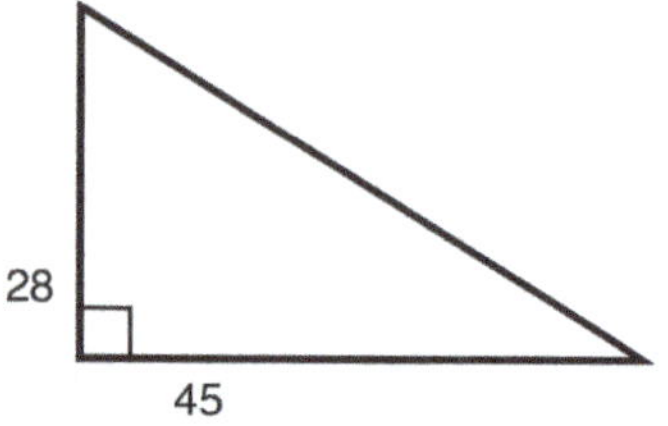

GOOD
JOB!

SET 2

Find the distance between the points

Name:

Date: Score:

1.
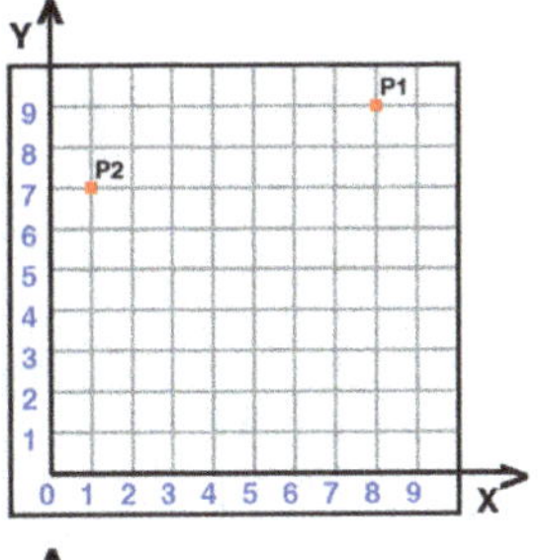

2.
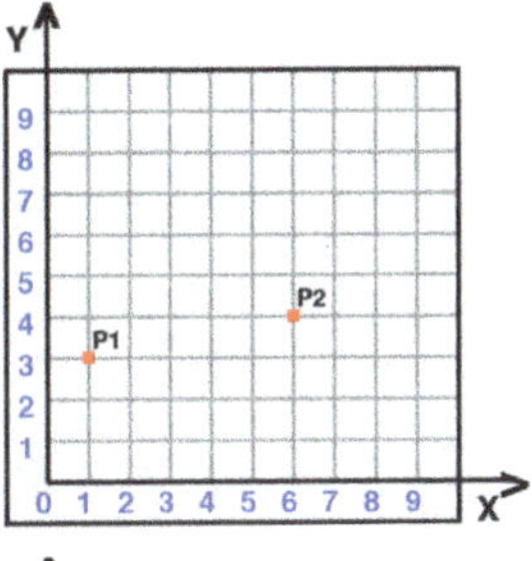

3.
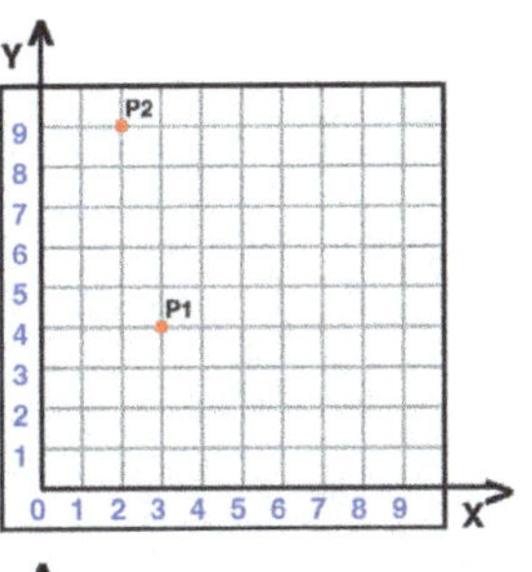

4.
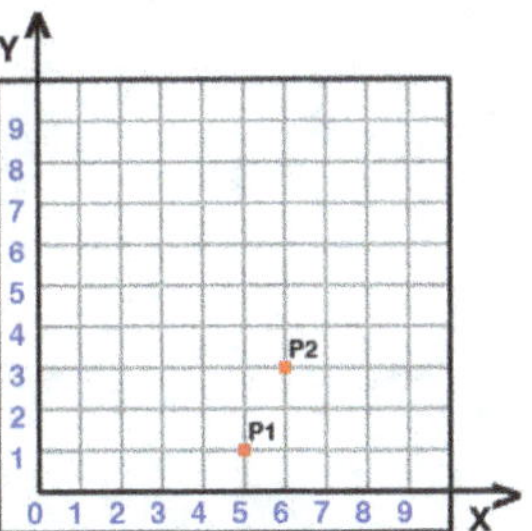

Name:

Date:

Score:

1.

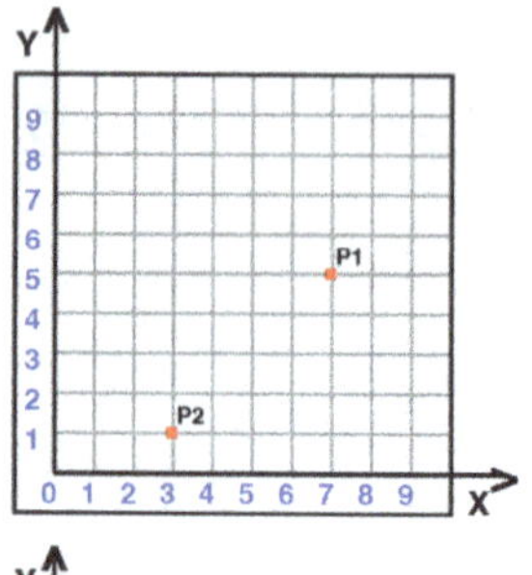

2.

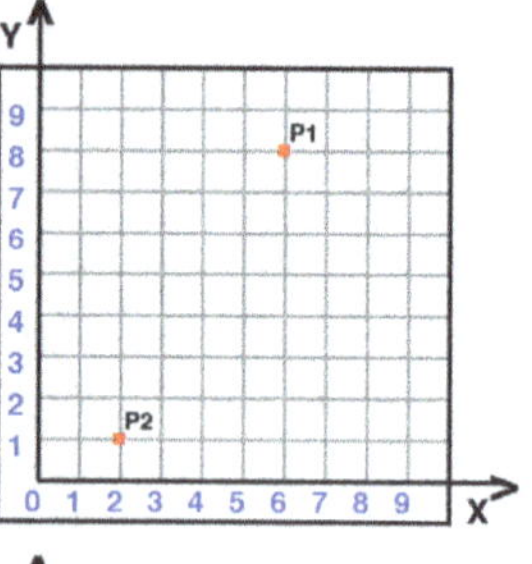

3.

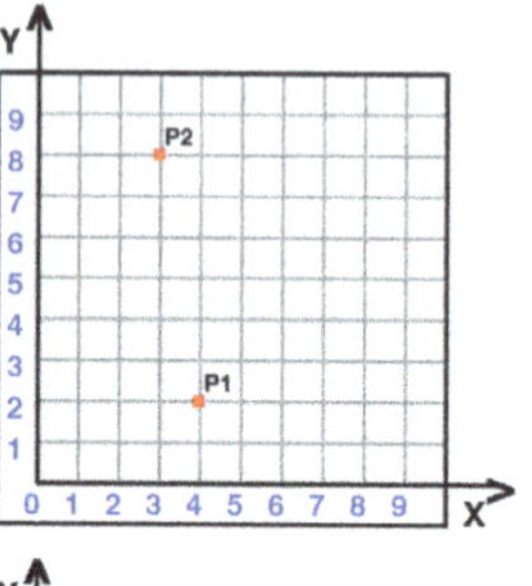

4.

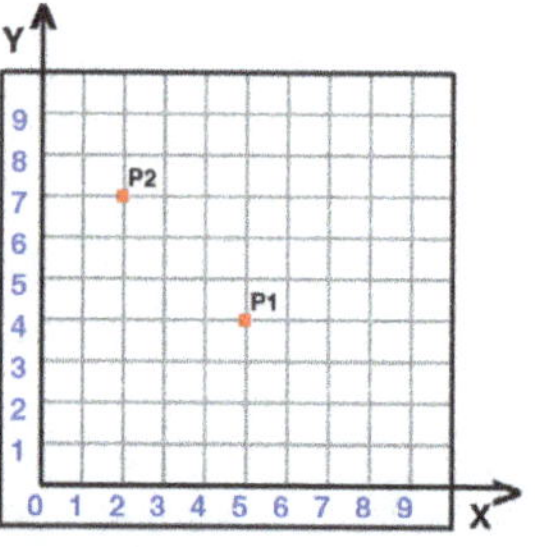

Name:

Date:

Score:

1.

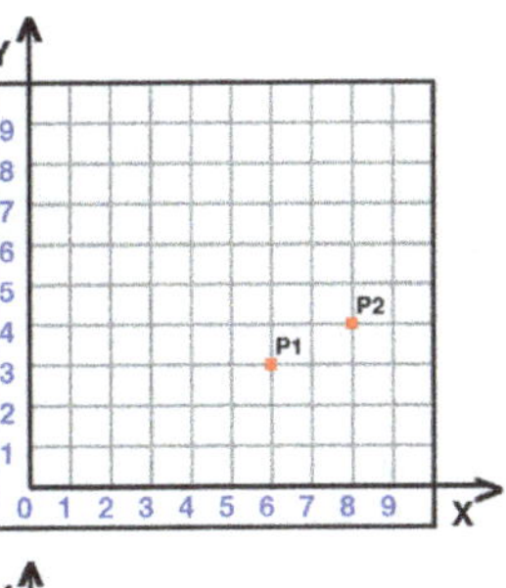

2.

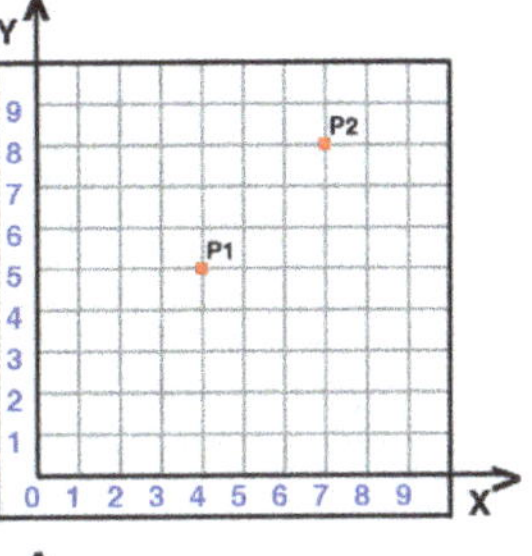

3.

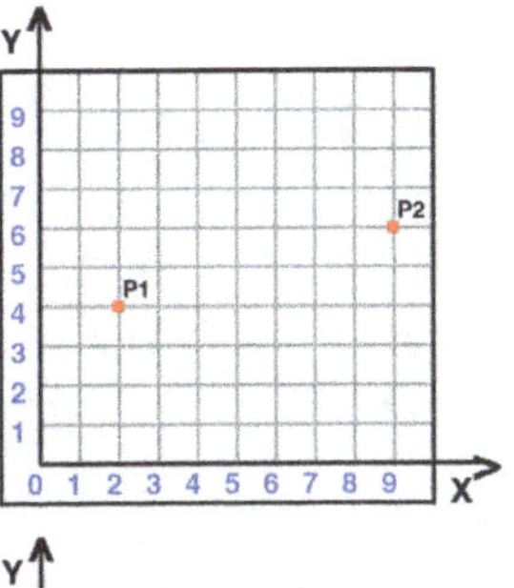

4.

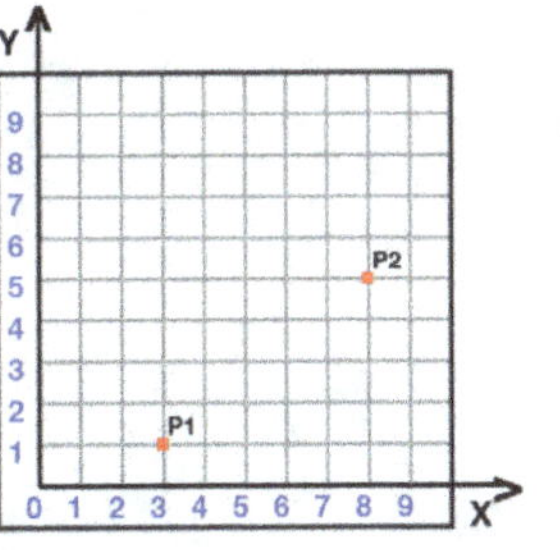

Name: _______________________

Date: _______________________   Score: _______________________

1.
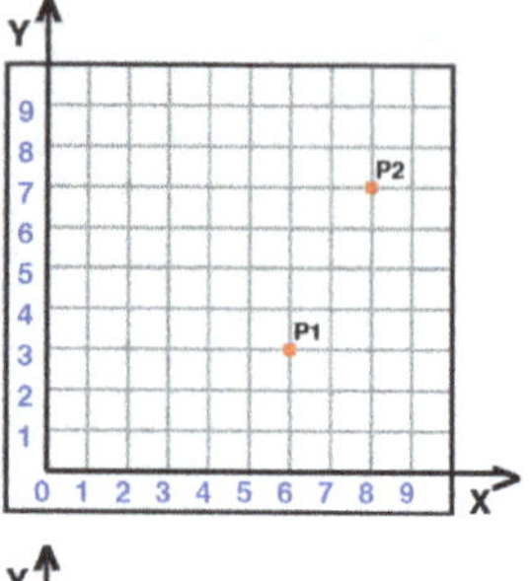

2.
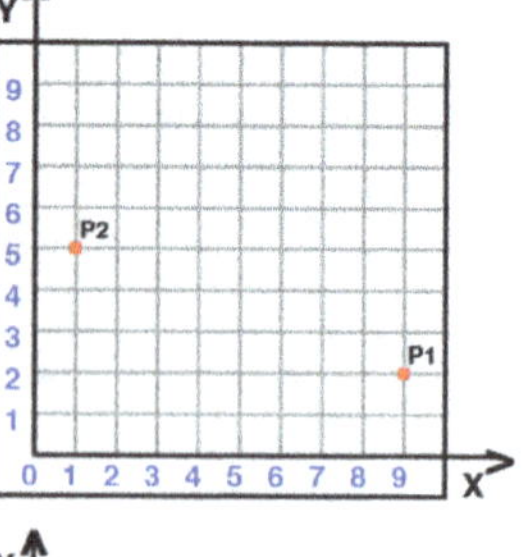

3.
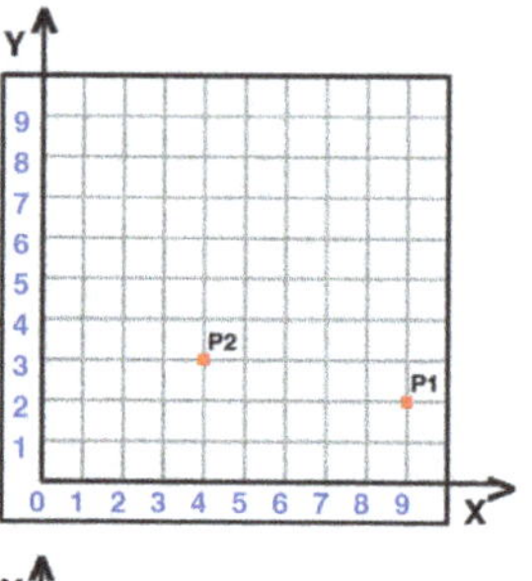

4.
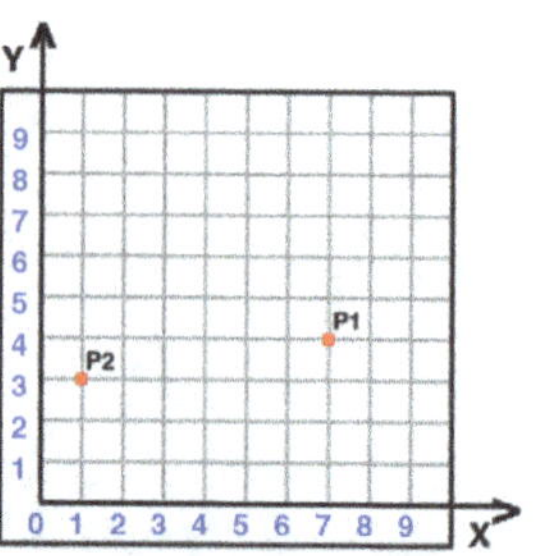

EXERCISE NO. 5

Name:

Date: Score:

1.

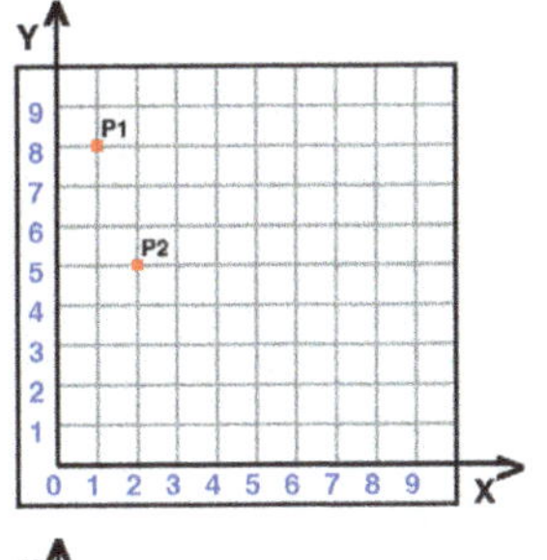

2.

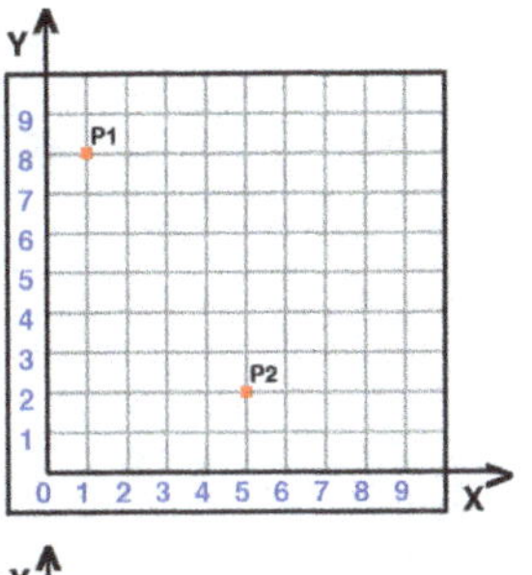

3.

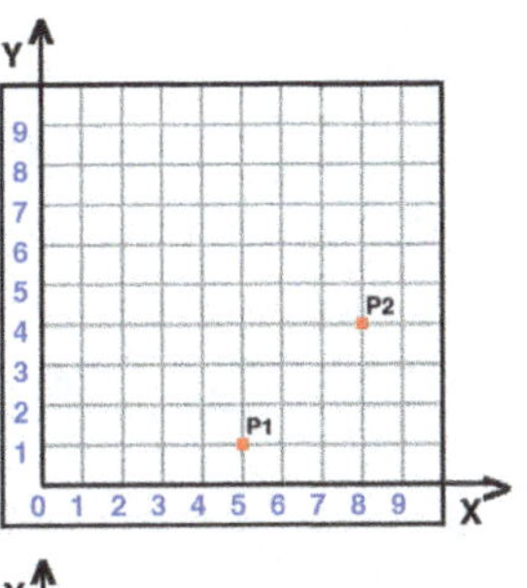

4.

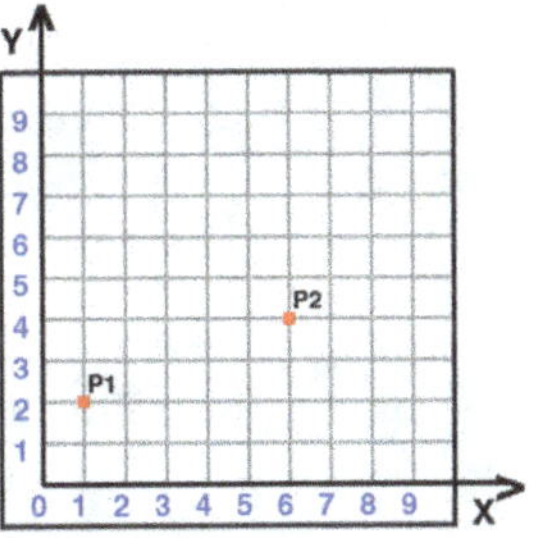

Name:

Date:

Score:

1. 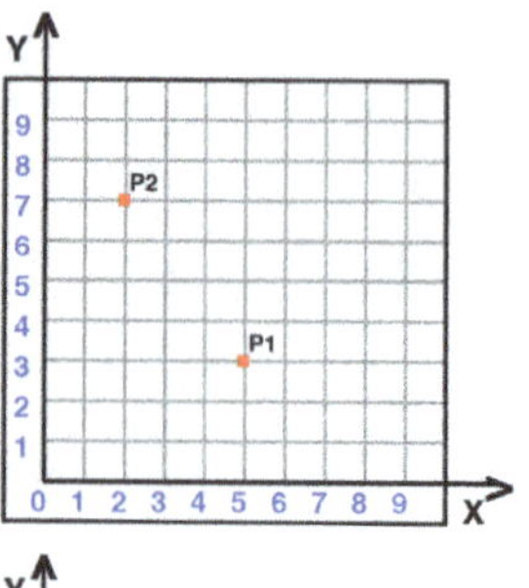

2. 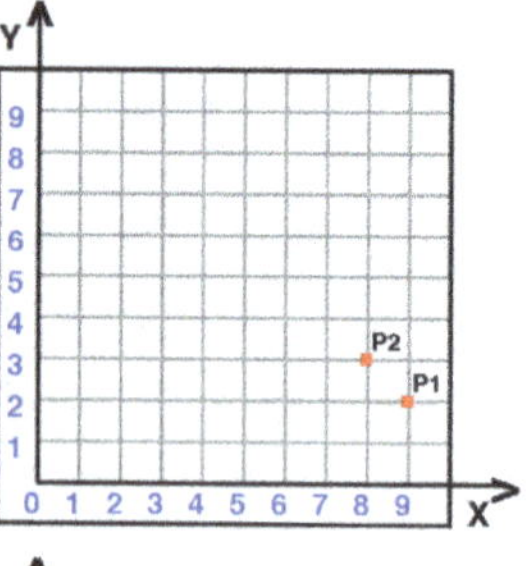

3. 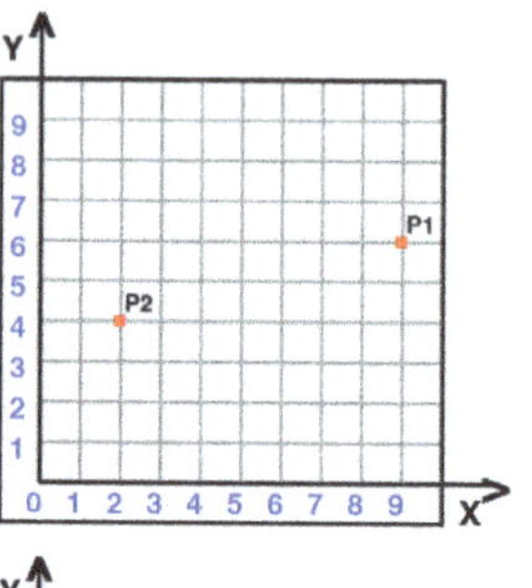

4. 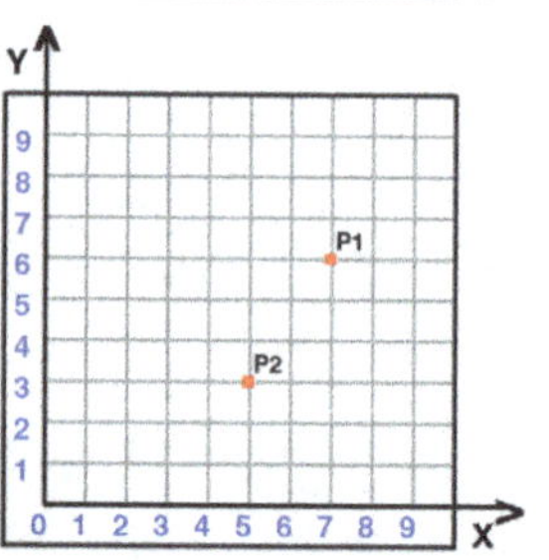

Name:

Date: Score:

1.

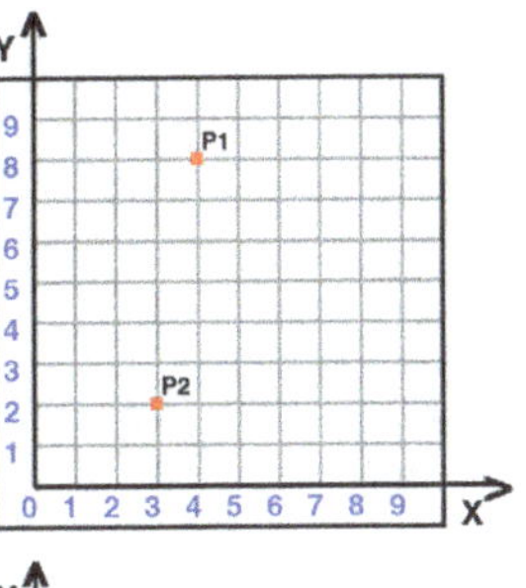

2.

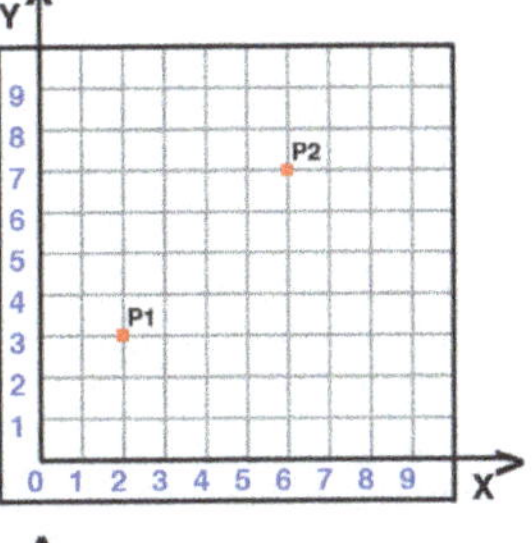

3.

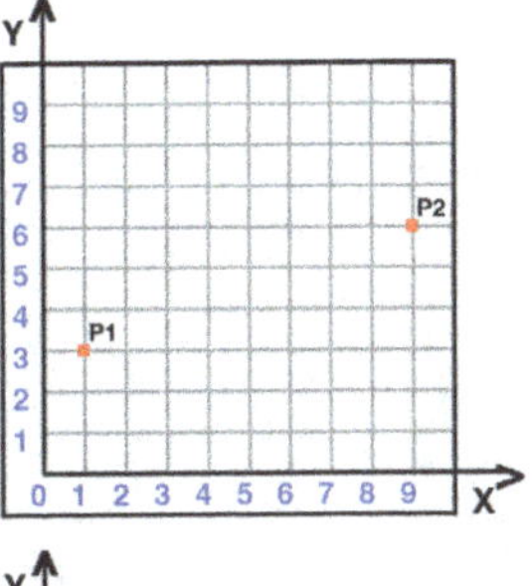

4.

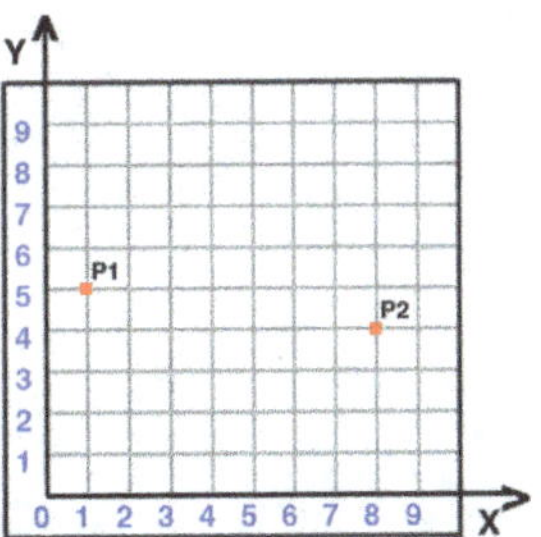

Name:

Date:

Score:

1.

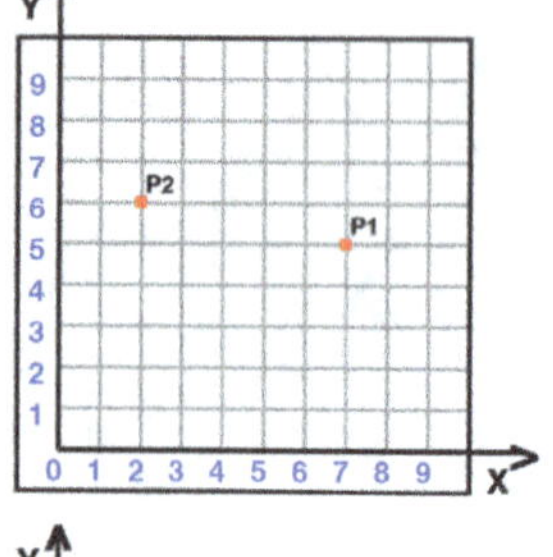

2.

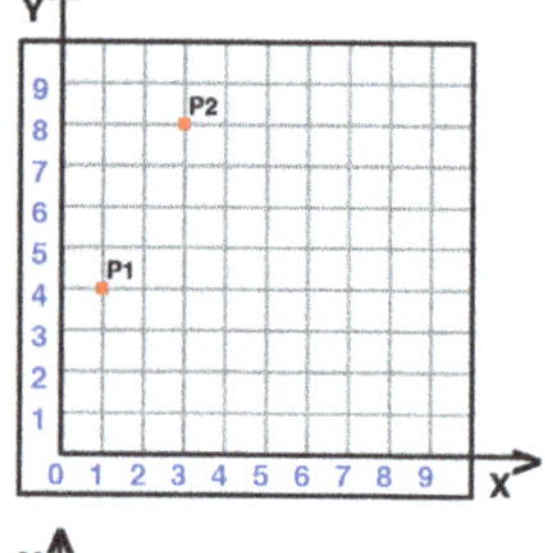

3.

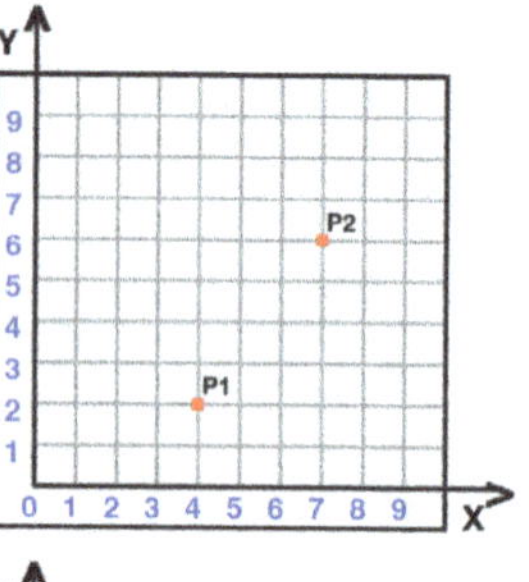

4.

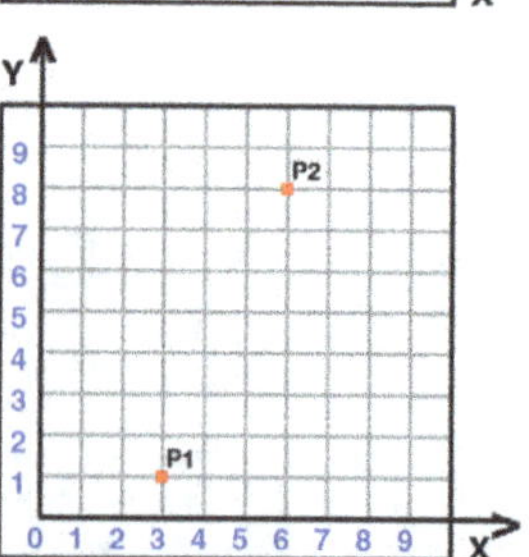

Name:

Date:

Score:

1.

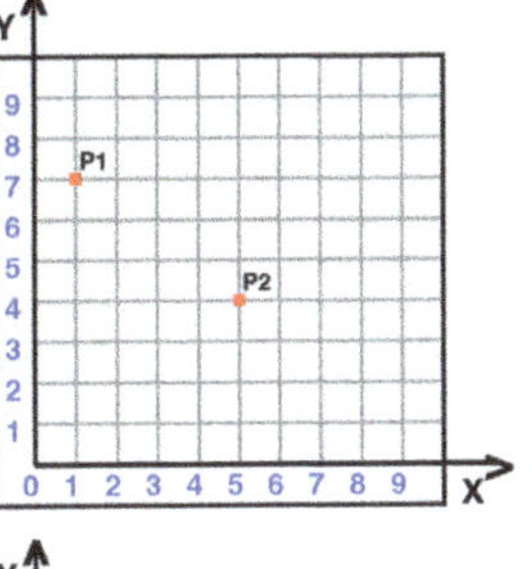

2.

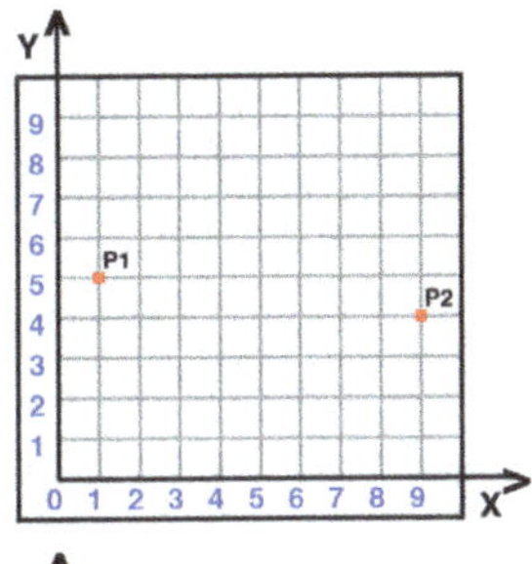

3.

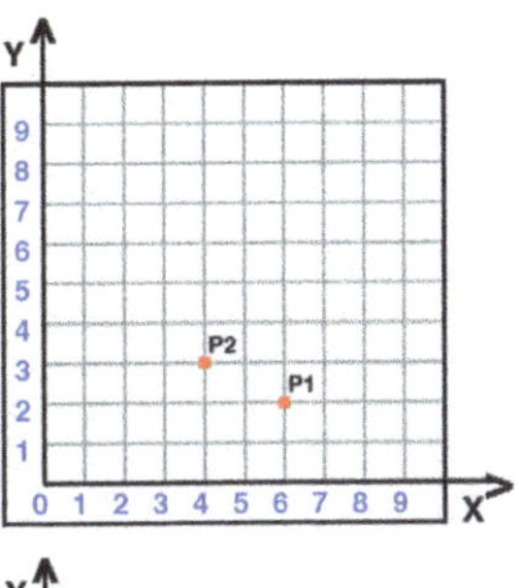

4.

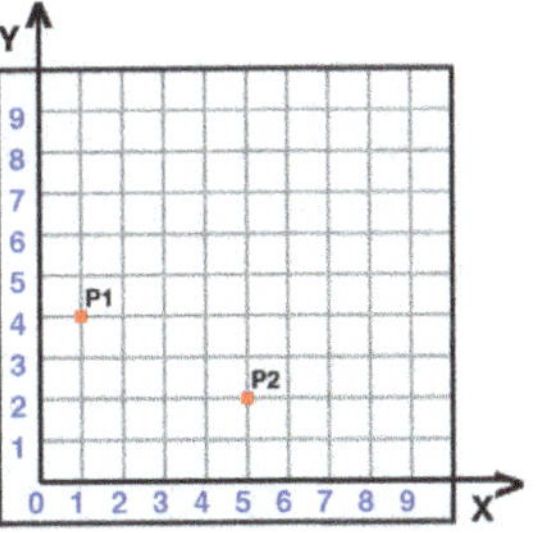

Name: ....

Date: ....   Score: ....

1.

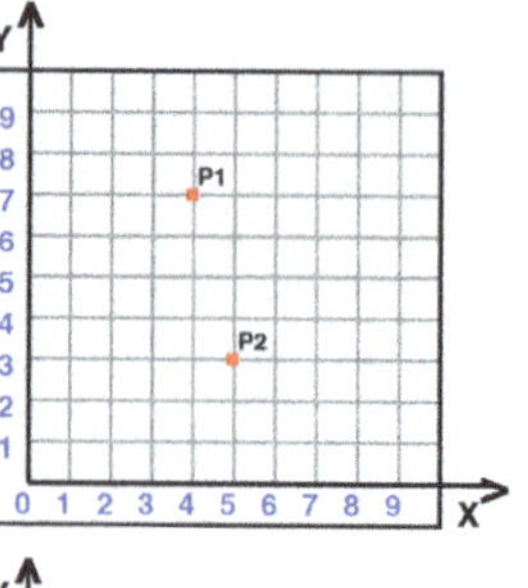

2.

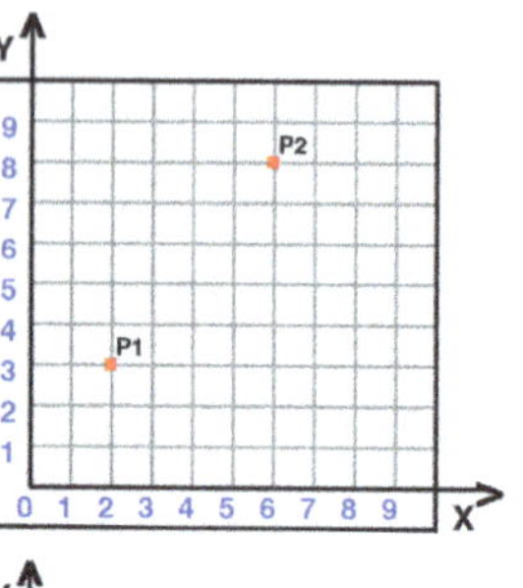

3.

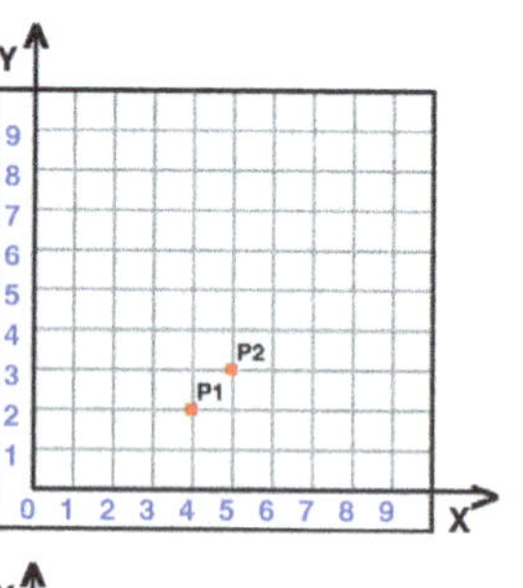

4.

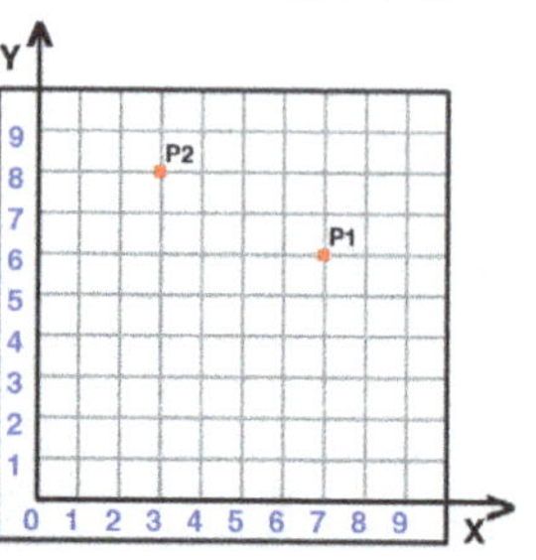

Name:

Date:

Score:

1. 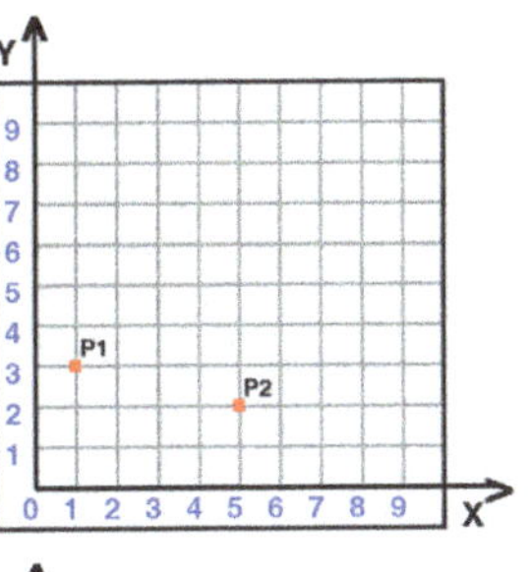

2. 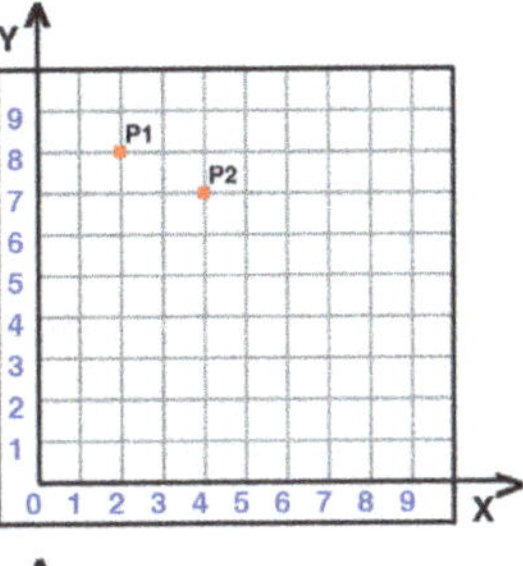

3. 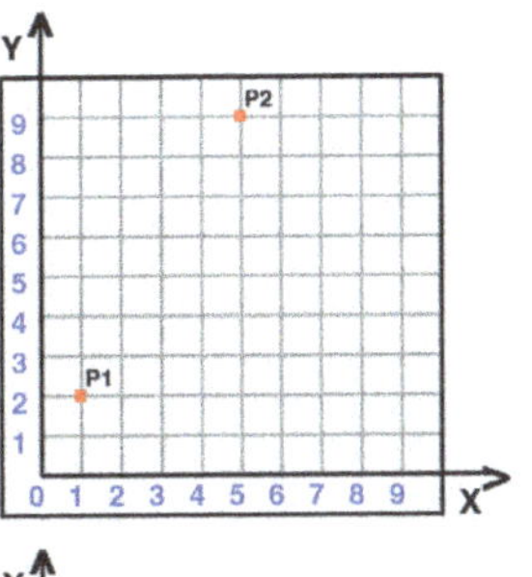

4. 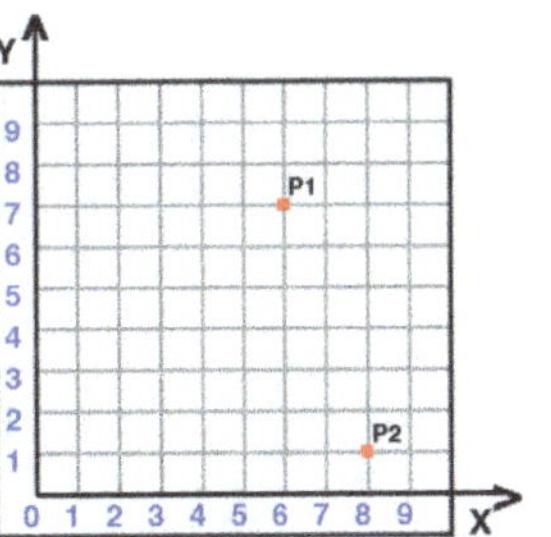

Name:

Date:

Score:

1.

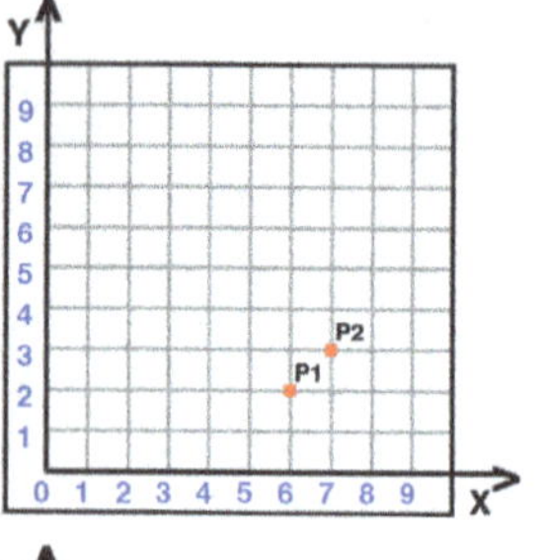

2.

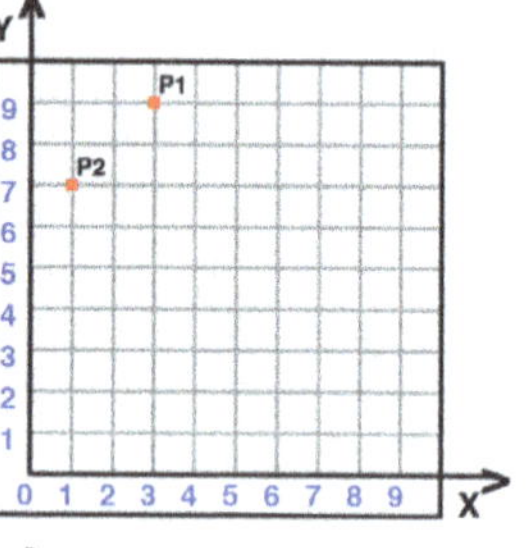

3.

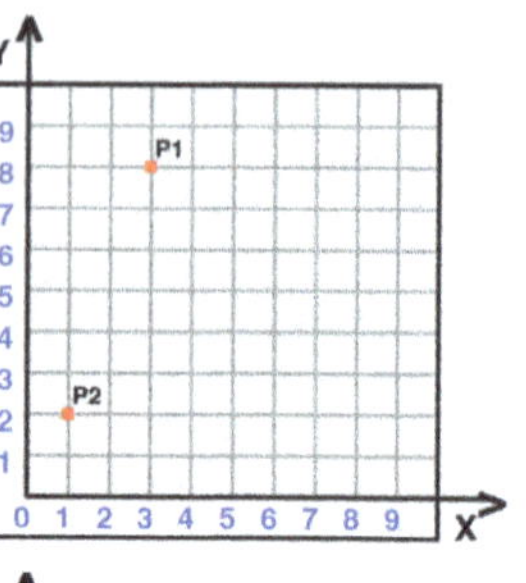

4.

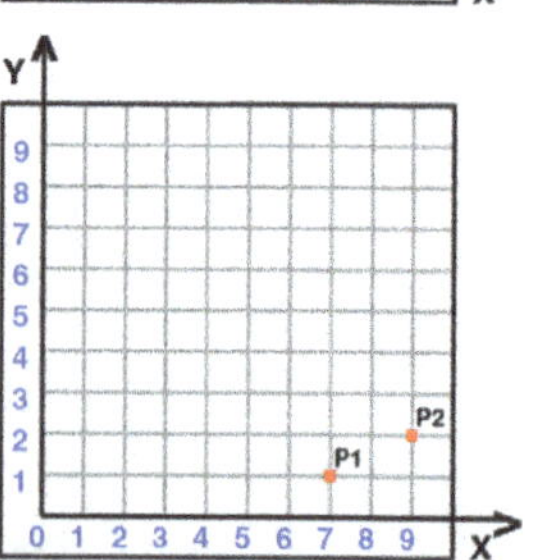

Name:

Date: Score:

1. 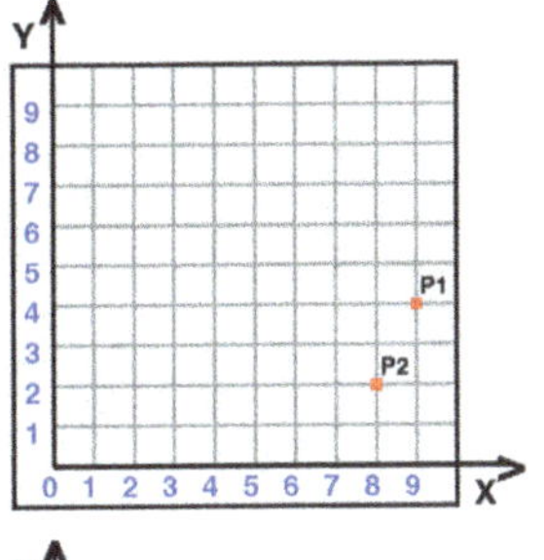

2. 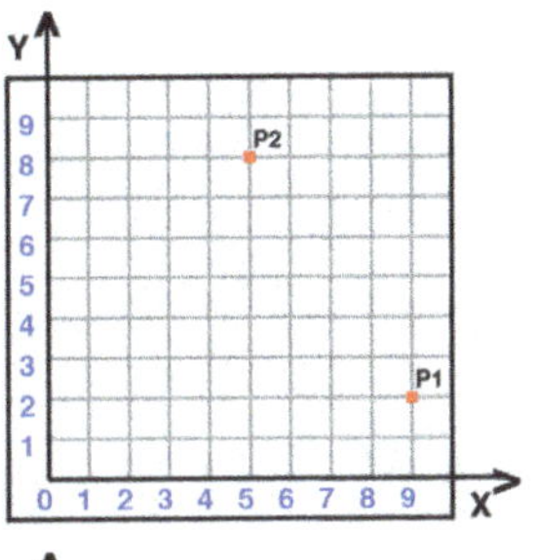

3. 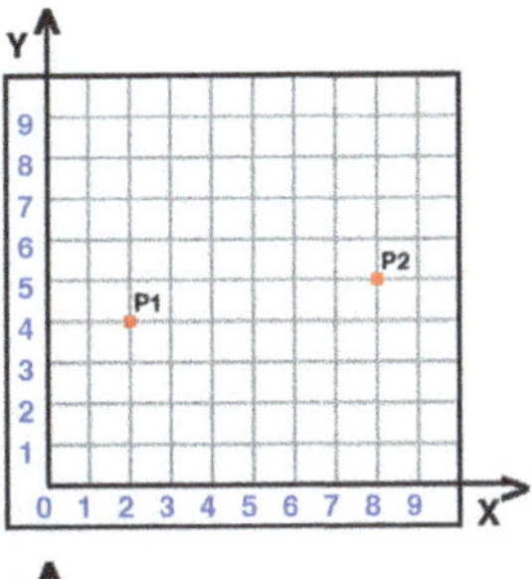

4. 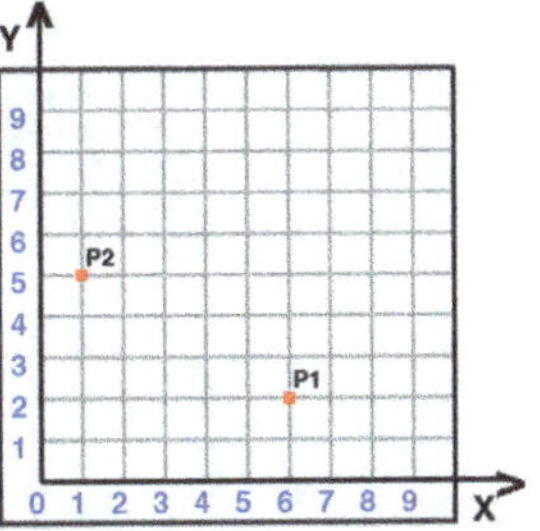

Name:

Date: Score:

1. 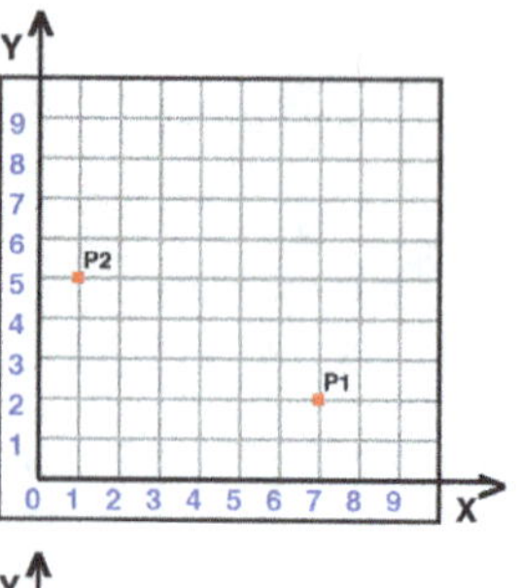

2. 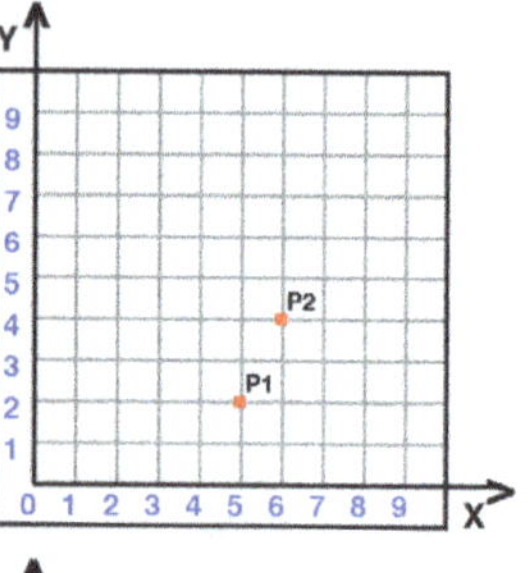

3. 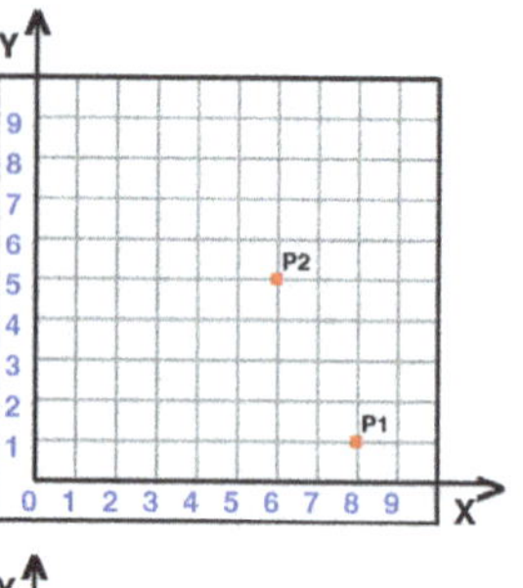

4. 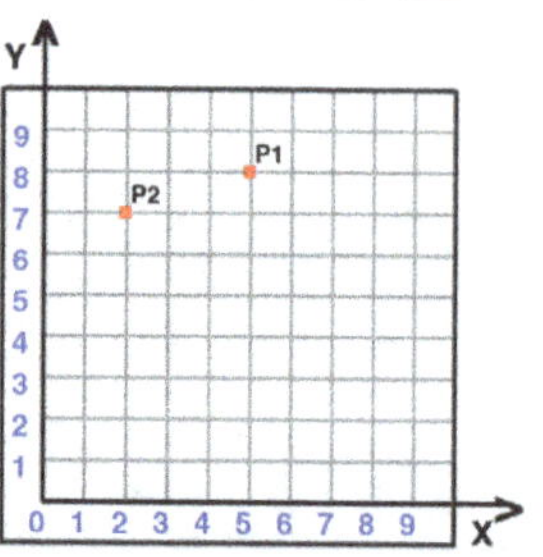

Name:

Date: Score:

1.
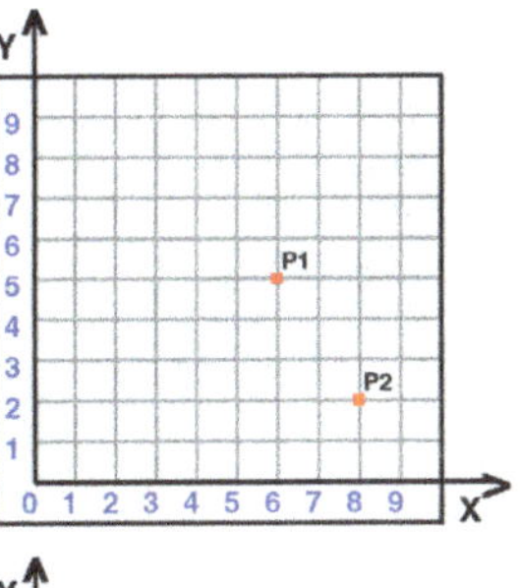

2.
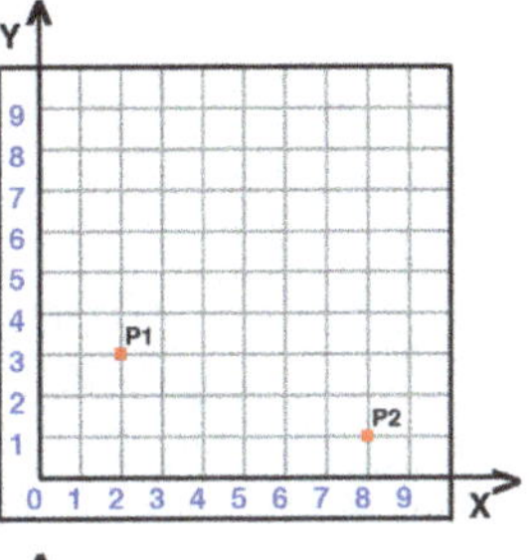

3.
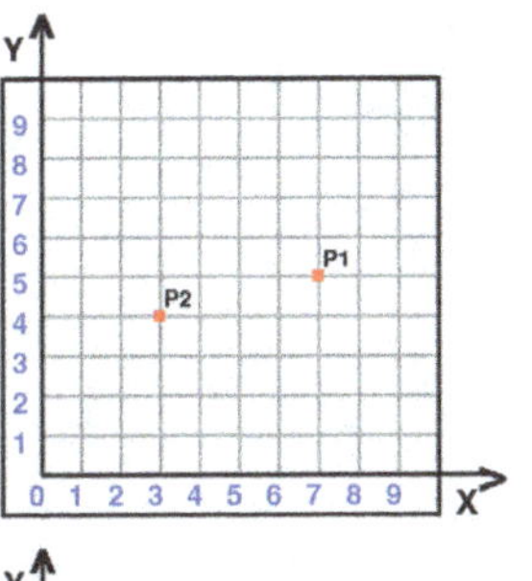

4.
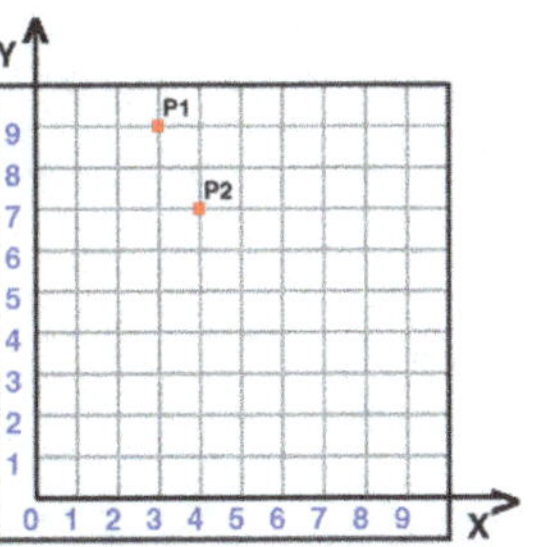

Excellent!

SET 3

Find the measure of the missing angle.

Name:

Date:

Score:

1.
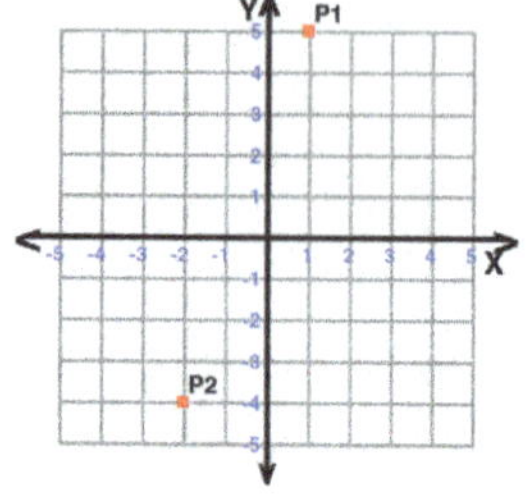

2.
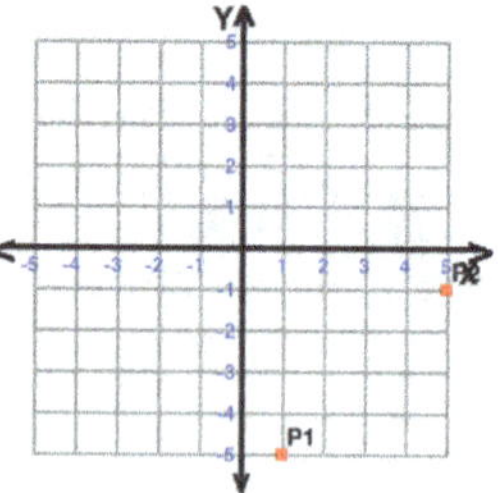

3.
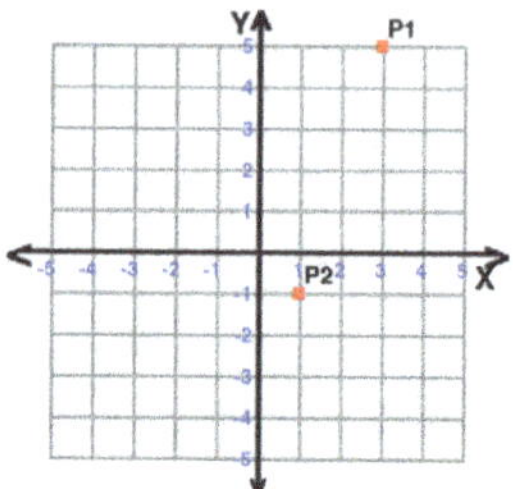

4.
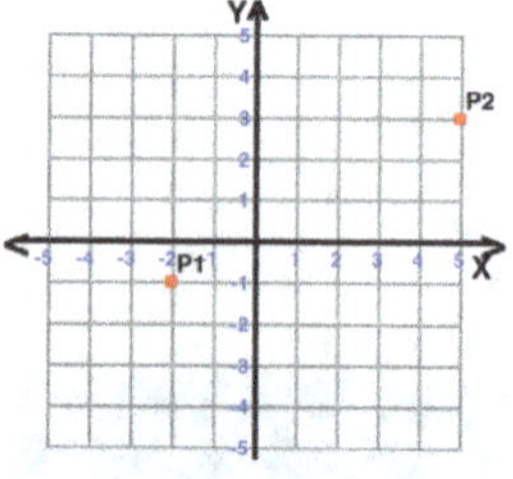

Name:

Date:

Score:

1.

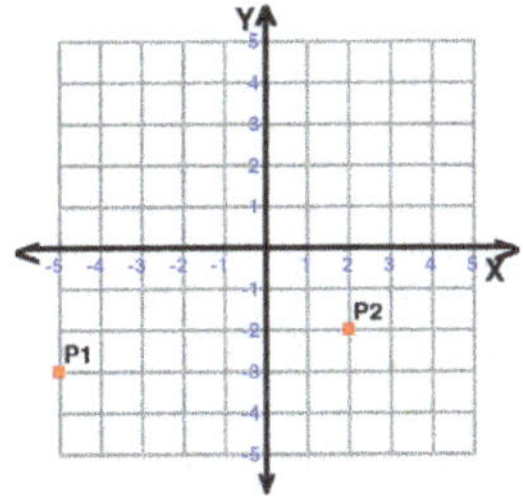

2.

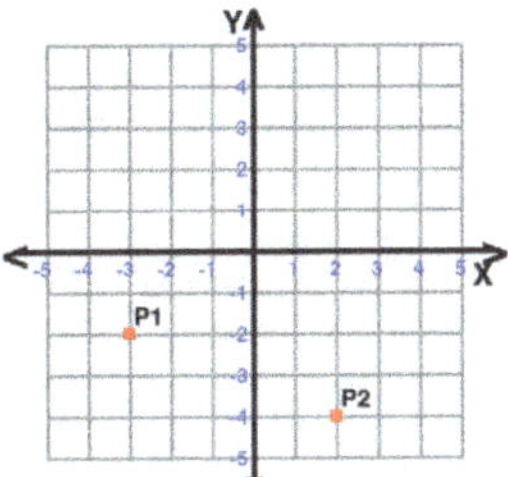

3.

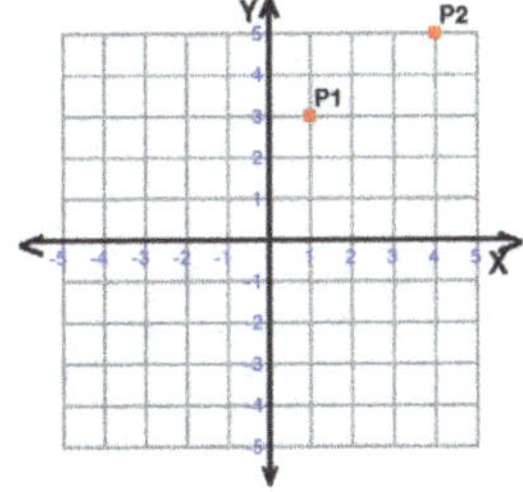

4.

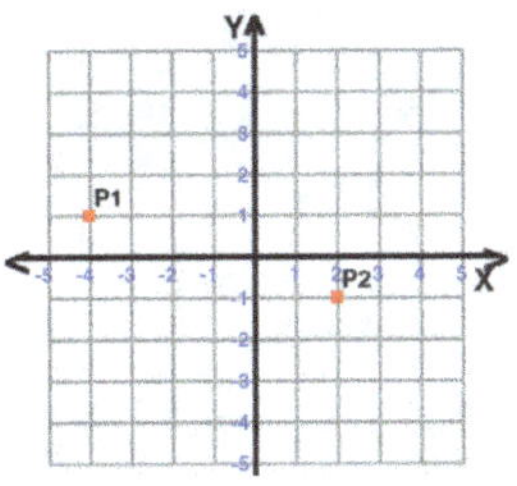

Name:

Date:

Score:

1.

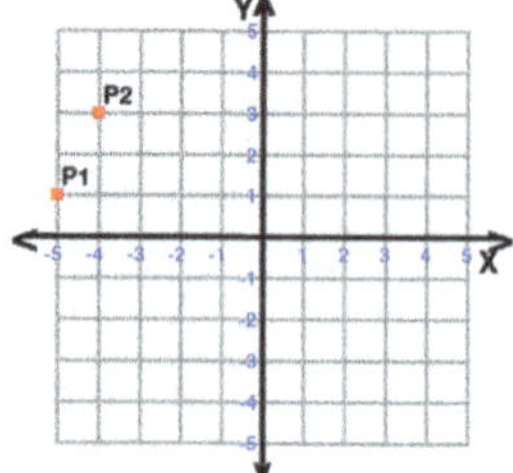

2.

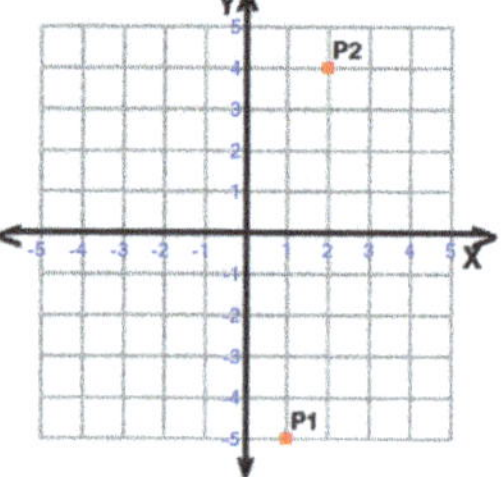

3.

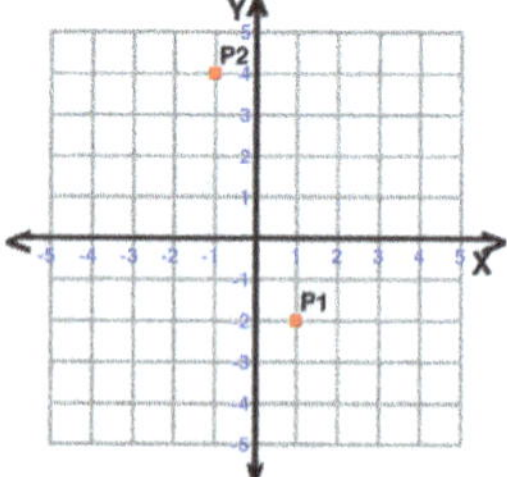

4.

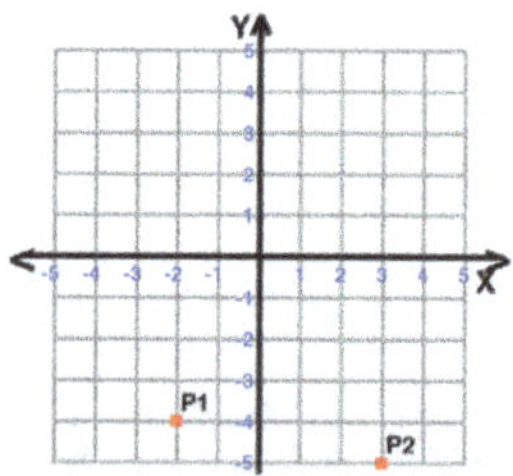

Name:

Date:

Score:

1.

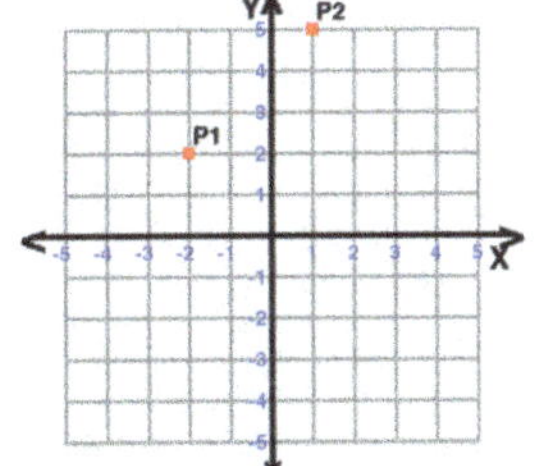

2.

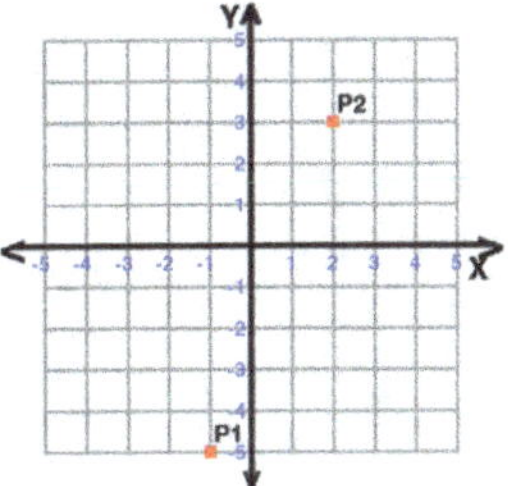

3.

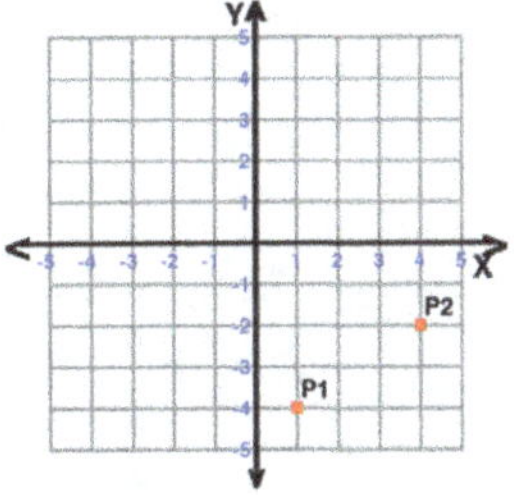

4.

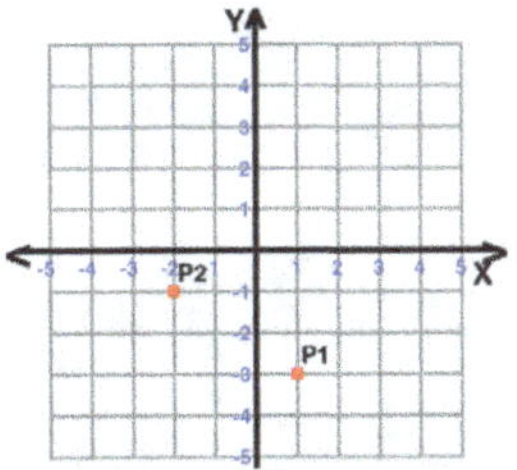

Name:

Date:

Score:

1. 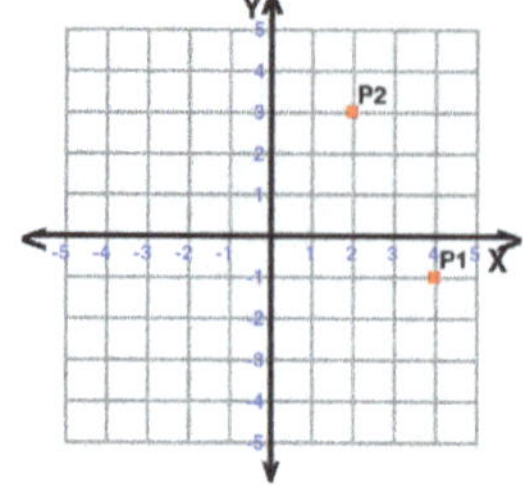

2. 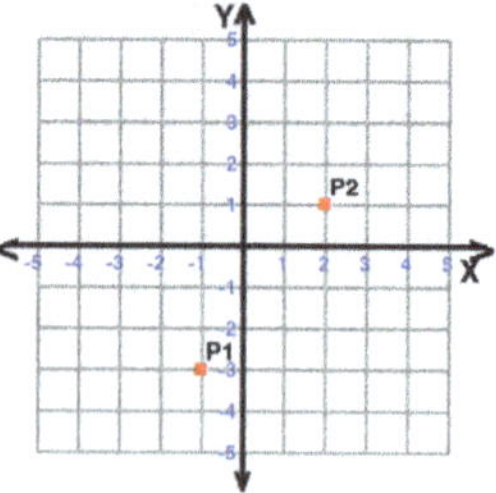

3. 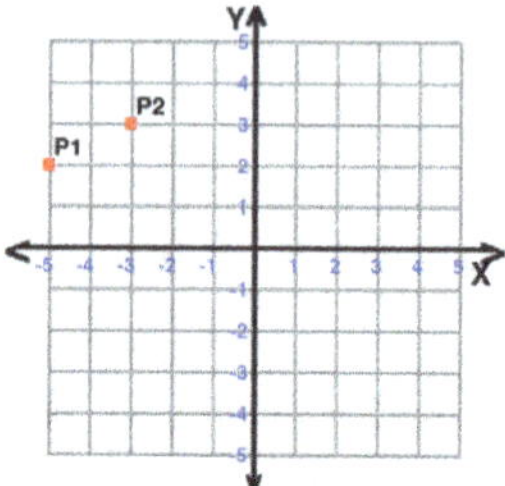

4. 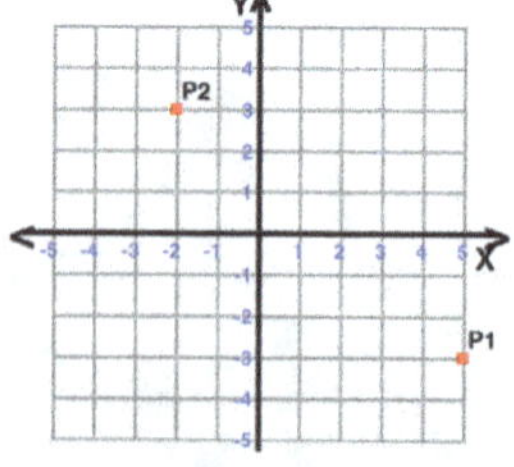

Name: ....

Date: ....

Score: ....

1.
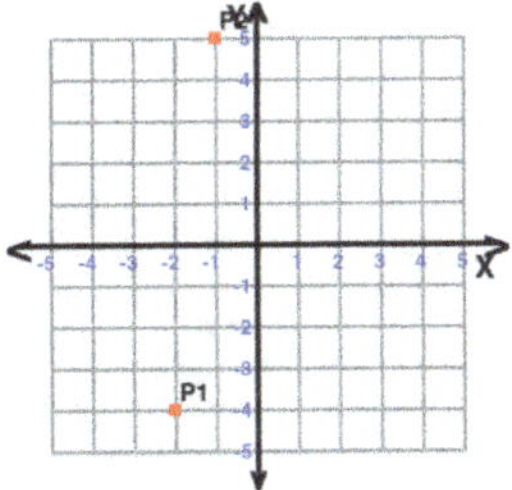

2.
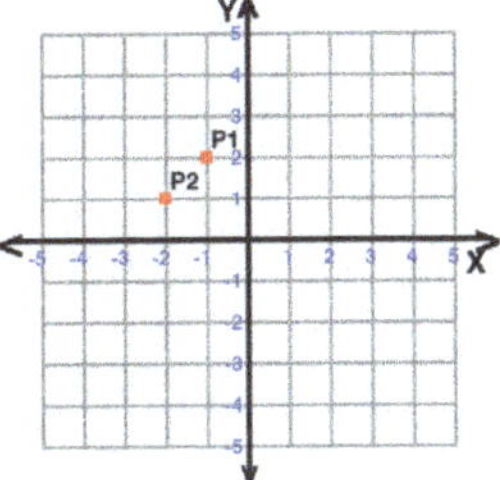

3.
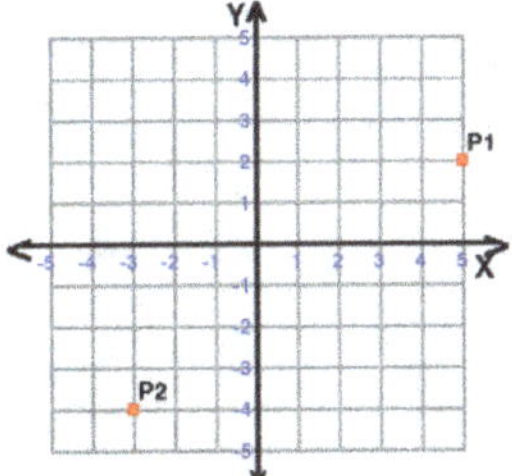

4.
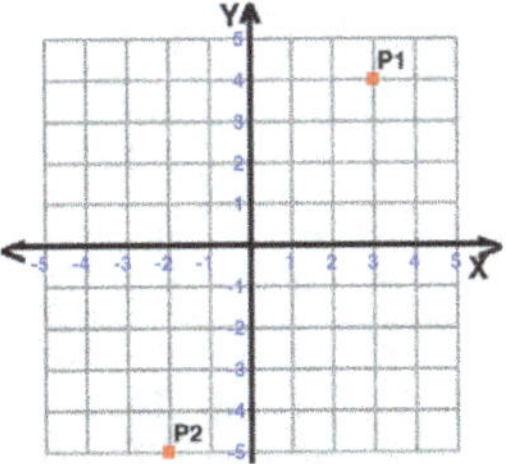

Name:

Date: Score:

1.

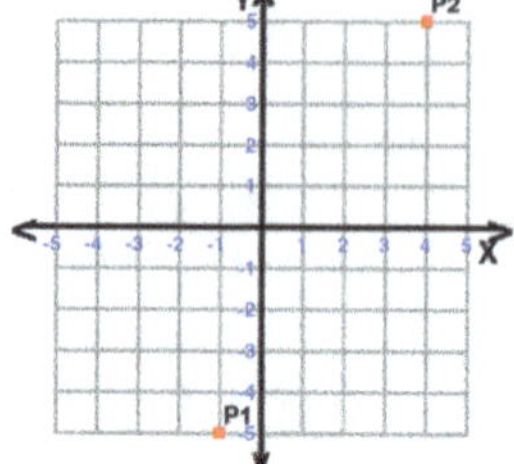

2.

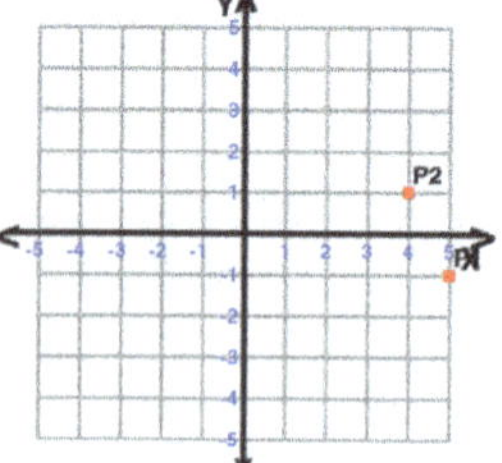

3.

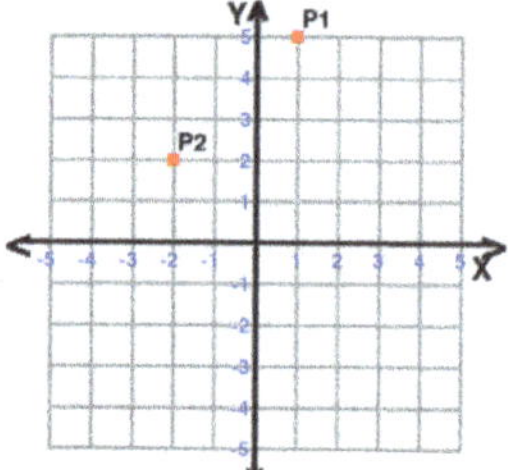

4.

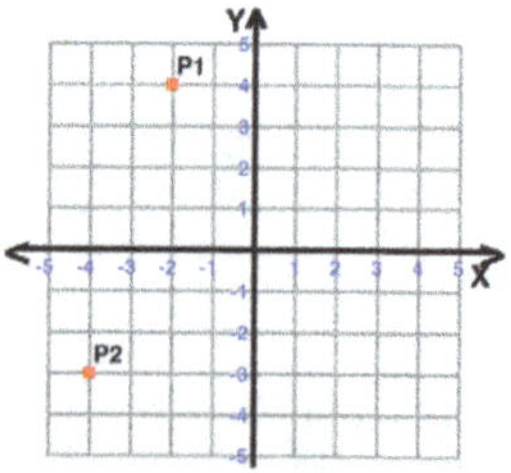

Name:

Date: Score:

1.
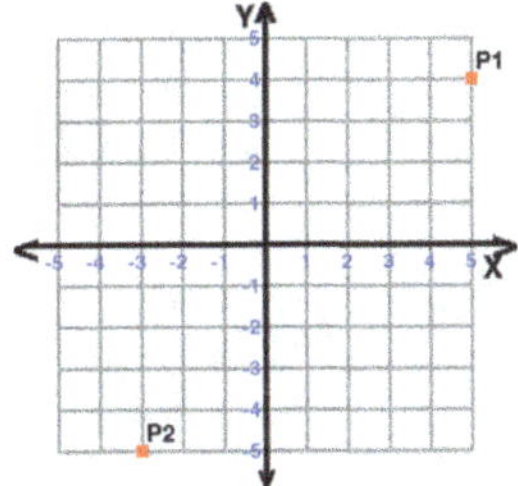

2.
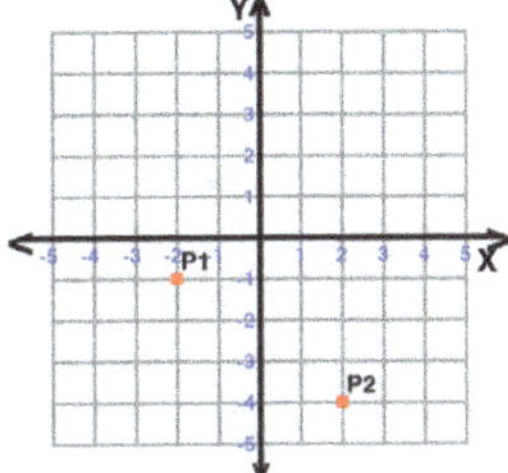

3.
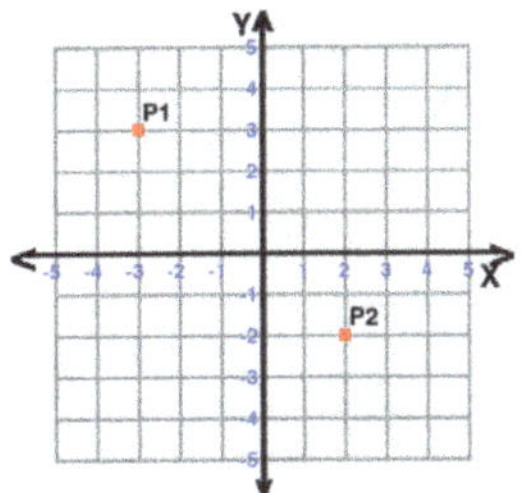

4.
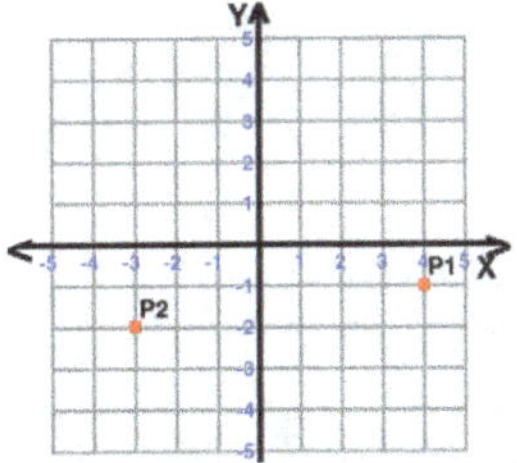

Name:

Date:

Score:

1. 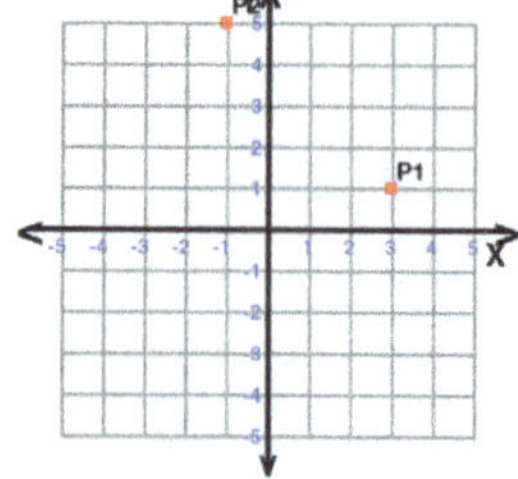

2. 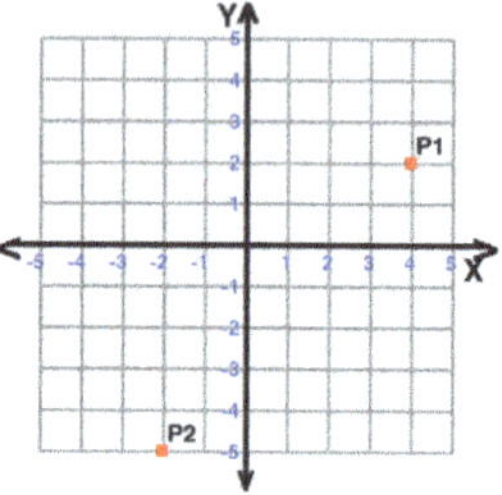

3. 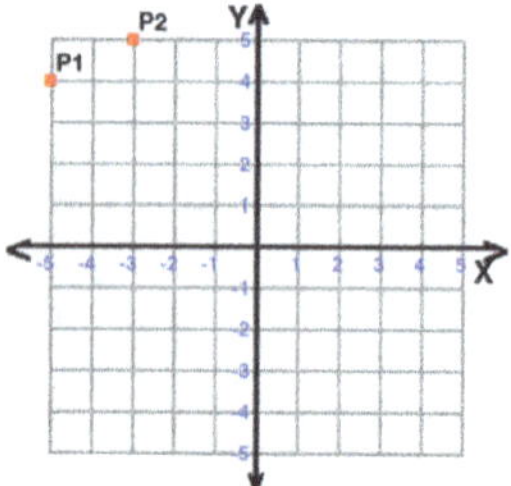

4. 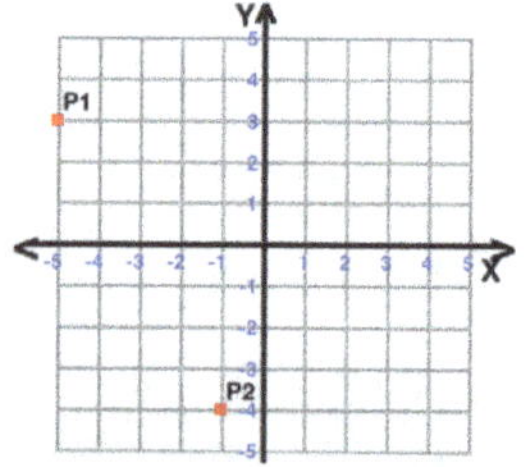

Name: ....

Date: ....

Score: ....

1.

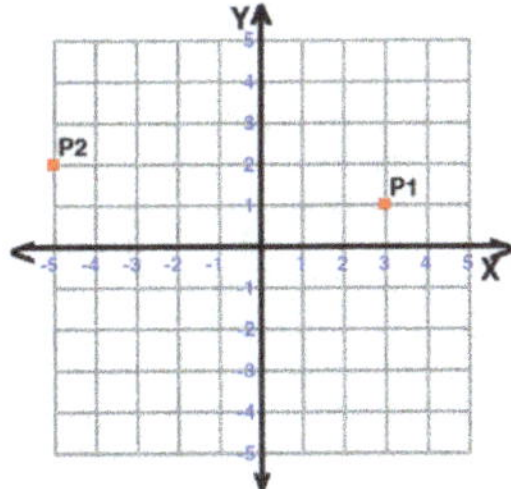

2.

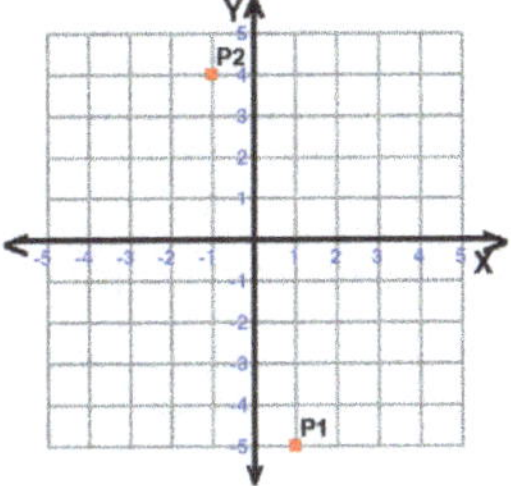

3.

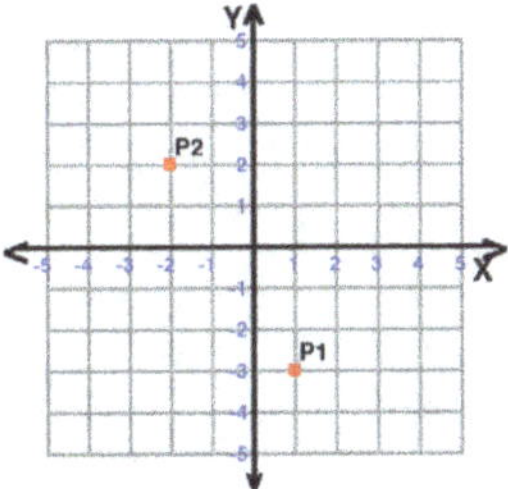

4.

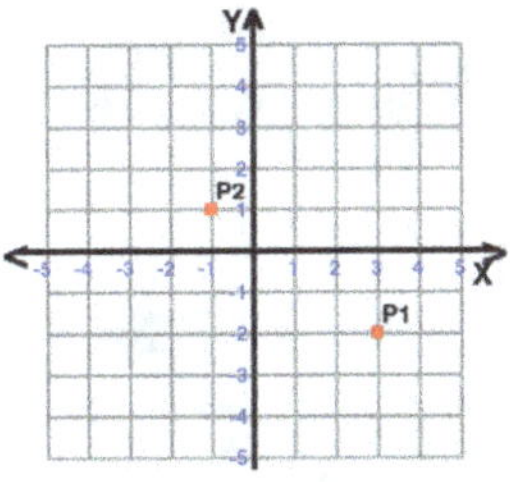

Name:

Date: Score:

1. 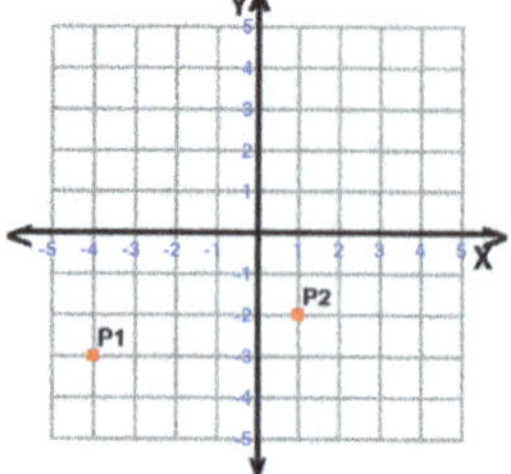

2. 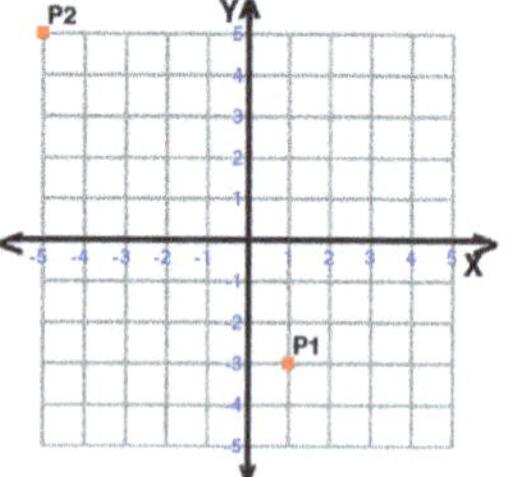

3. 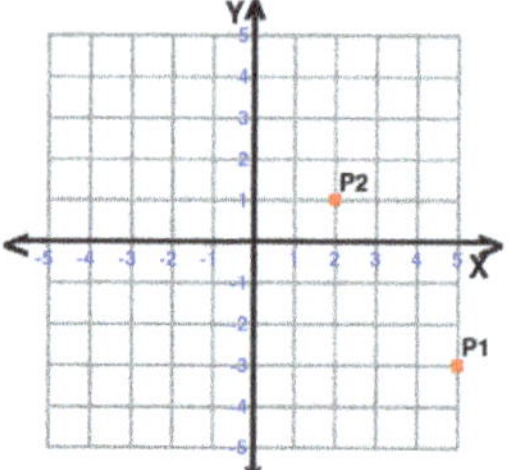

4. 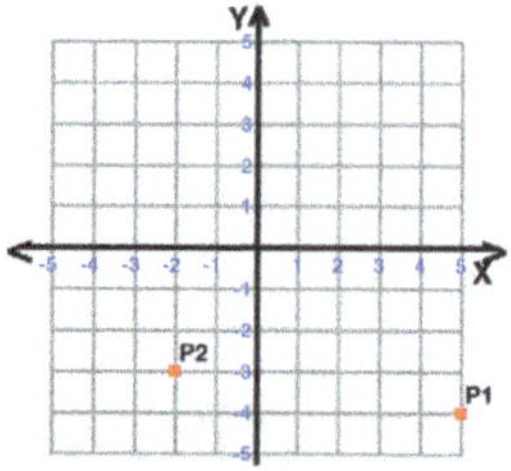

Name:

Date: Score:

1.
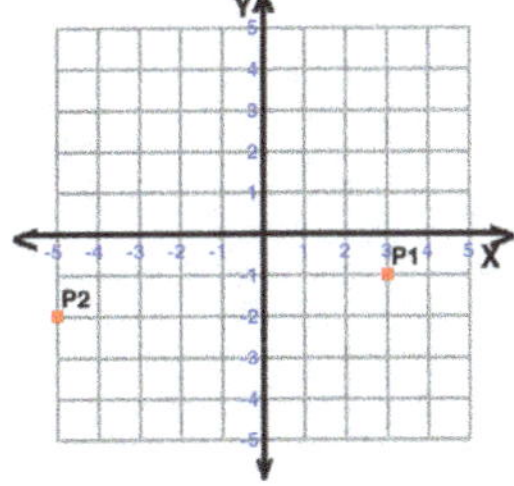

2.
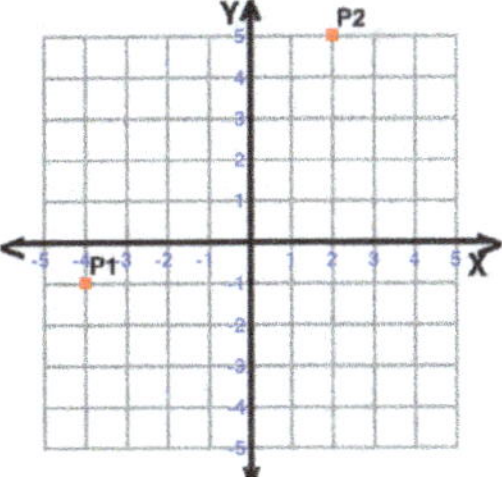

3.
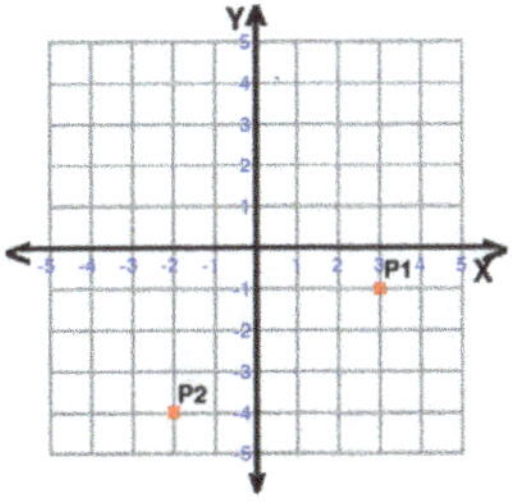

4.
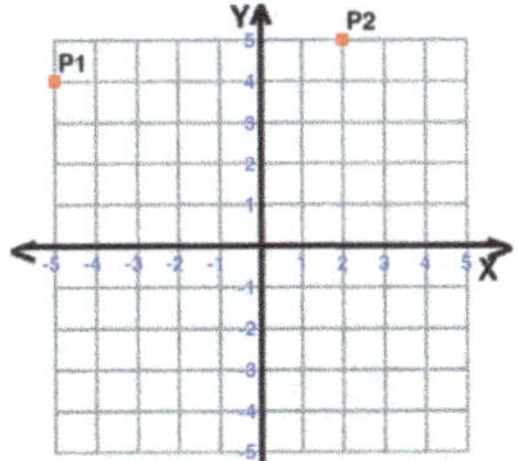

Name: ____________________

Date: ____________________   Score: ____________________

1. 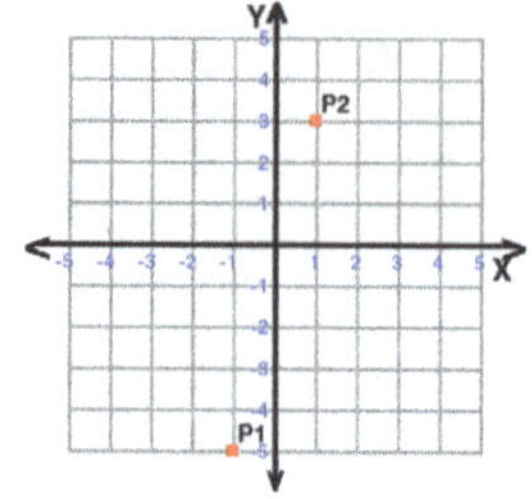

2. 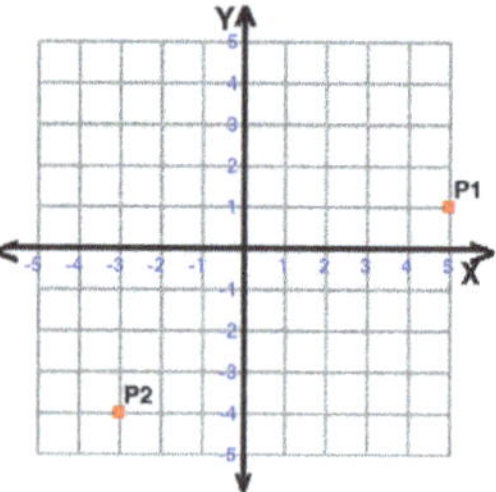

3. 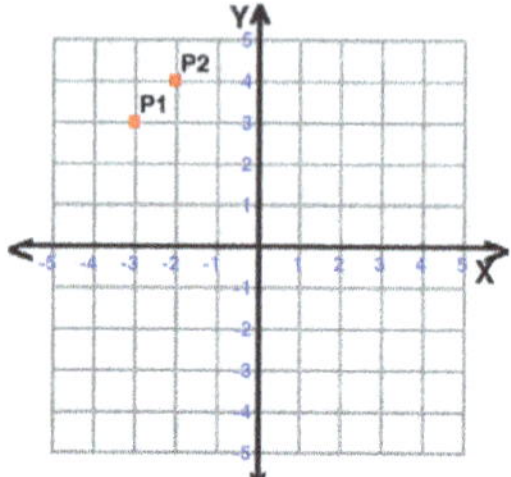

4. 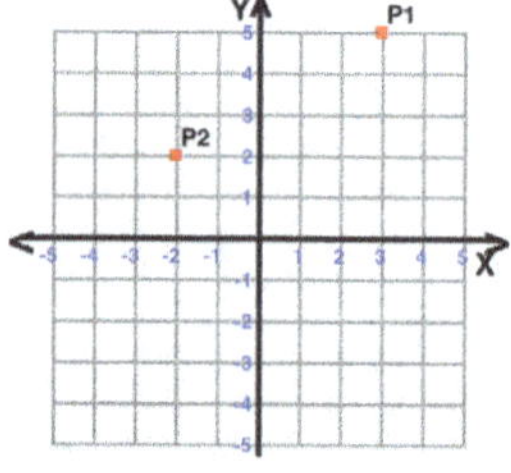

Name:

Date:

Score:

1.

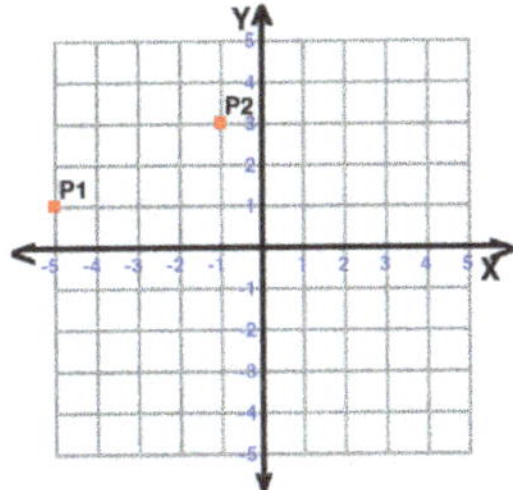

2.

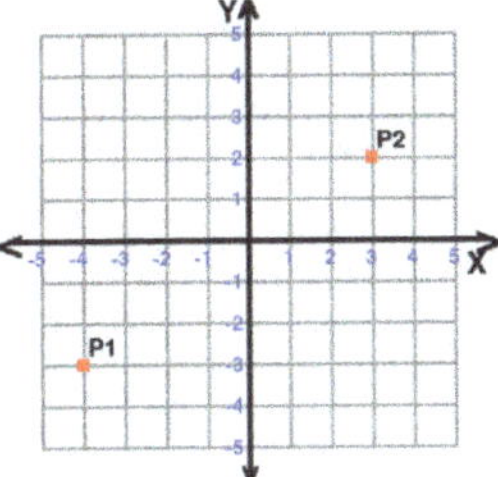

3.

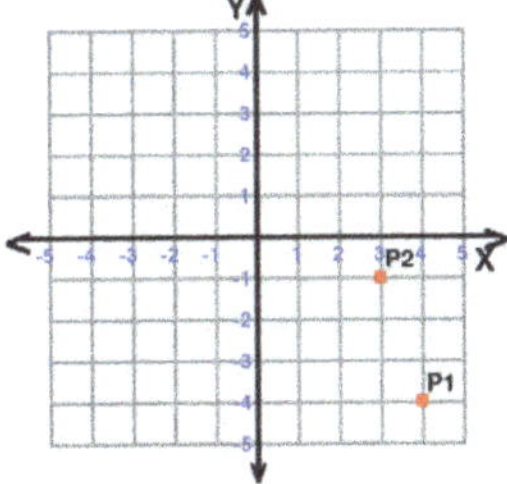

4.

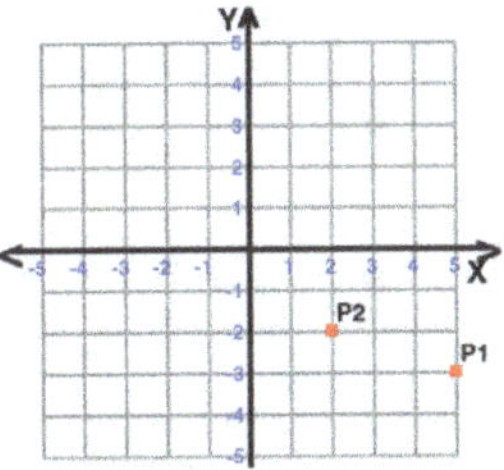

Name: ___________________________

Date: ___________________________   Score: ___________________________

1.

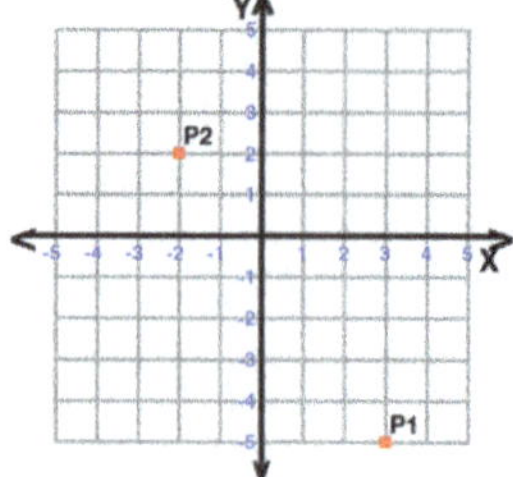

____

2.

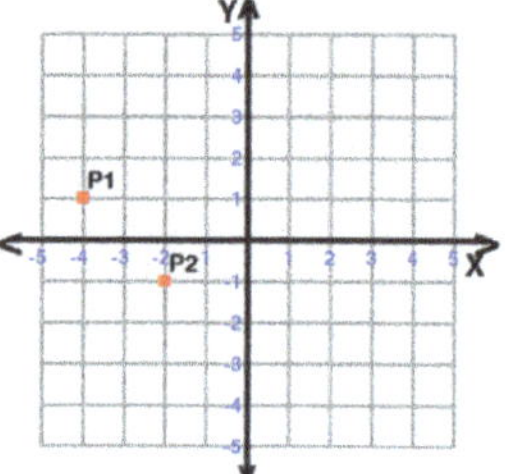

____

3.

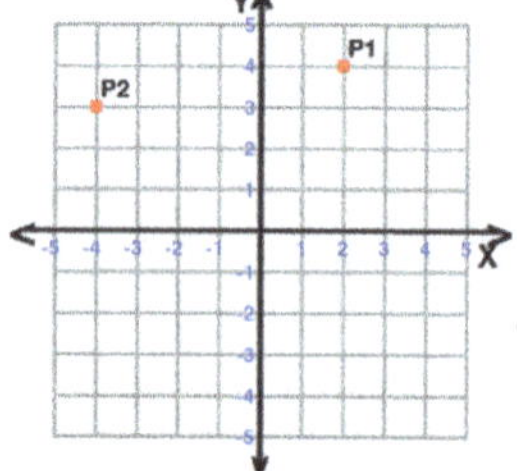

____

4.

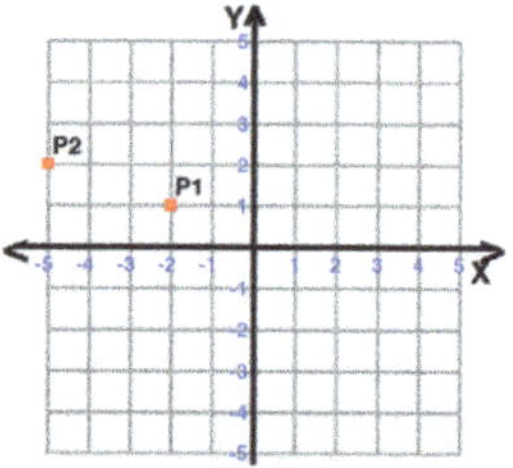

____

Great Job Kid!

AWESOME!

Learning Pythagorean Theorem is Fun Right? Keep on learning!

ANSWERS

SET 1

Find the length of the third side of each triangle

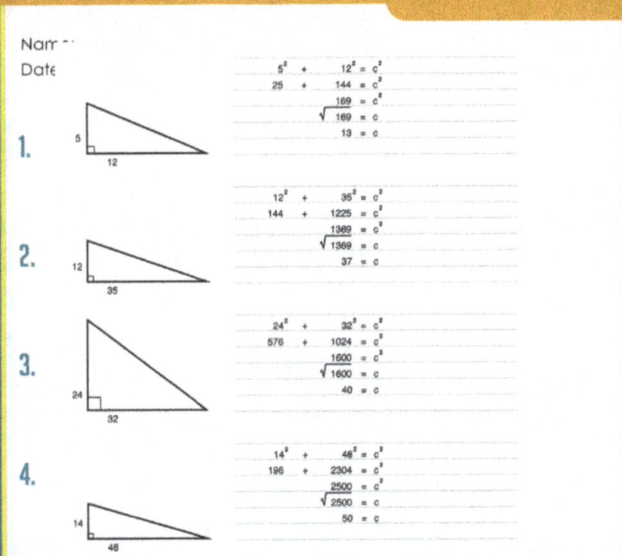

Name:
Date:

1.
$$5^2 + 12^2 = c^2$$
$$25 + 144 = c^2$$
$$169 = c^2$$
$$\sqrt{169} = c$$
$$13 = c$$

2.
$$12^2 + 35^2 = c^2$$
$$144 + 1225 = c^2$$
$$1369 = c^2$$
$$\sqrt{1369} = c$$
$$37 = c$$

3.
$$24^2 + 32^2 = c^2$$
$$576 + 1024 = c^2$$
$$1600 = c^2$$
$$\sqrt{1600} = c$$
$$40 = c$$

4.
$$14^2 + 48^2 = c^2$$
$$196 + 2304 = c^2$$
$$2500 = c^2$$
$$\sqrt{2500} = c$$
$$50 = c$$

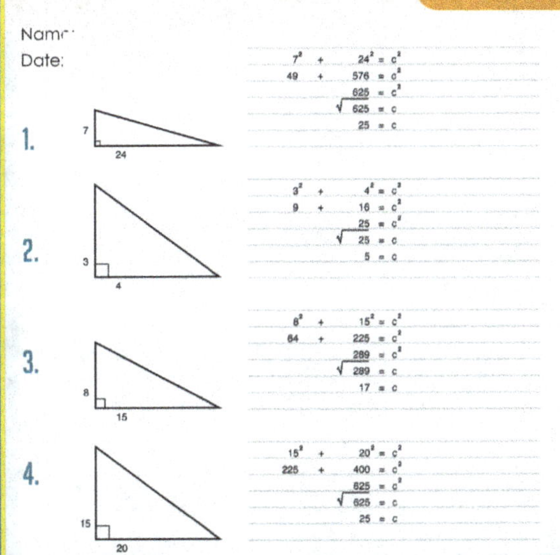

Name:
Date:

1.
$$7^2 + 24^2 = c^2$$
$$49 + 576 = c^2$$
$$625 = c^2$$
$$\sqrt{625} = c$$
$$25 = c$$

2.
$$3^2 + 4^2 = c^2$$
$$9 + 16 = c^2$$
$$25 = c^2$$
$$\sqrt{25} = c$$
$$5 = c$$

3.
$$8^2 + 15^2 = c^2$$
$$64 + 225 = c^2$$
$$289 = c^2$$
$$\sqrt{289} = c$$
$$17 = c$$

4.
$$15^2 + 20^2 = c^2$$
$$225 + 400 = c^2$$
$$625 = c^2$$
$$\sqrt{625} = c$$
$$25 = c$$

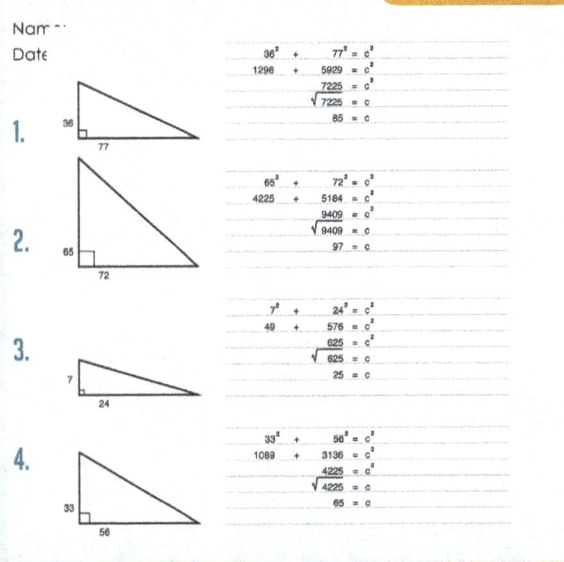

Name:
Date:

1.
$$36^2 + 77^2 = c^2$$
$$1296 + 5929 = c^2$$
$$7225 = c^2$$
$$\sqrt{7225} = c$$
$$85 = c$$

2.
$$65^2 + 72^2 = c^2$$
$$4225 + 5184 = c^2$$
$$9409 = c^2$$
$$\sqrt{9409} = c$$
$$97 = c$$

3.
$$7^2 + 24^2 = c^2$$
$$49 + 576 = c^2$$
$$625 = c^2$$
$$\sqrt{625} = c$$
$$25 = c$$

4.
$$33^2 + 56^2 = c^2$$
$$1089 + 3136 = c^2$$
$$4225 = c^2$$
$$\sqrt{4225} = c$$
$$65 = c$$

Name:
Date:

1. 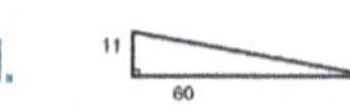

$$11^2 + 60^2 = c^2$$
$$121 + 3600 = c^2$$
$$3721 = c^2$$
$$\sqrt{3721} = c$$
$$61 = c$$

2. 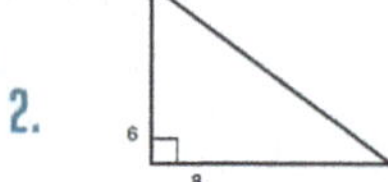

$$6^2 + 8^2 = c^2$$
$$36 + 64 = c^2$$
$$100 = c^2$$
$$\sqrt{100} = c$$
$$10 = c$$

3. 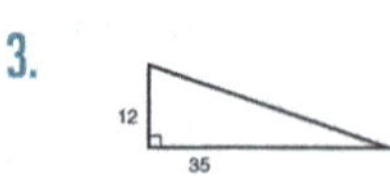

$$12^2 + 35^2 = c^2$$
$$144 + 1225 = c^2$$
$$1369 = c^2$$
$$\sqrt{1369} = c$$
$$37 = c$$

4. 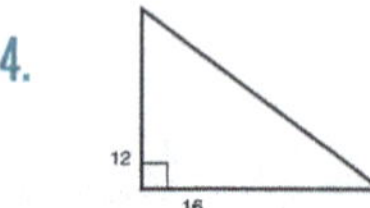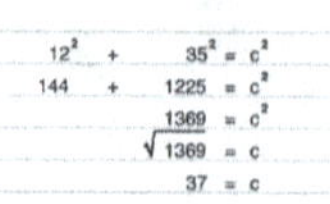

$$12^2 + 16^2 = c^2$$
$$144 + 256 = c^2$$
$$400 = c^2$$
$$\sqrt{400} = c$$
$$20 = c$$

Name:
Date:

1. 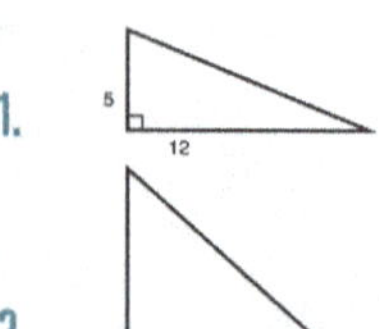

$$5^2 + 12^2 = c^2$$
$$25 + 144 = c^2$$
$$169 = c^2$$
$$\sqrt{169} = c$$
$$13 = c$$

2. 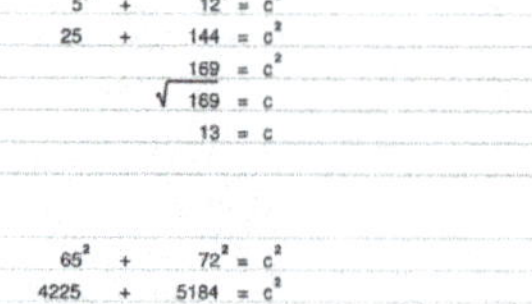

$$65^2 + 72^2 = c^2$$
$$4225 + 5184 = c^2$$
$$9409 = c^2$$
$$\sqrt{9409} = c$$
$$97 = c$$

3. 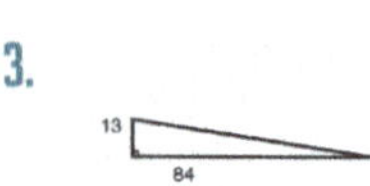

$$13^2 + 84^2 = c^2$$
$$169 + 7056 = c^2$$
$$7225 = c^2$$
$$\sqrt{7225} = c$$
$$85 = c$$

4. 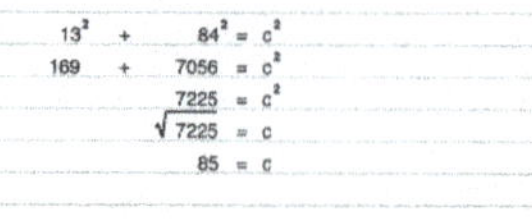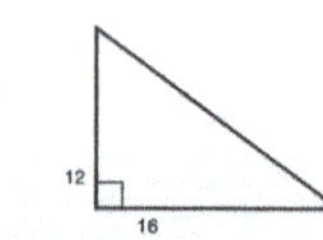

$$12^2 + 16^2 = c^2$$
$$144 + 256 = c^2$$
$$400 = c^2$$
$$\sqrt{400} = c$$
$$20 = c$$

Name:
Date: Score:

1. 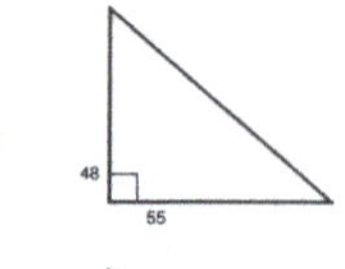

$$48^2 + 55^2 = c^2$$
$$2304 + 3025 = c^2$$
$$5329 = c^2$$
$$\sqrt{5329} = c$$
$$73 = c$$

2. 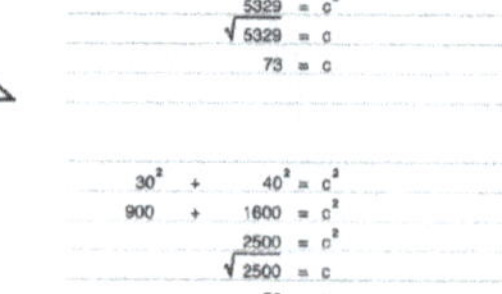

$$30^2 + 40^2 = c^2$$
$$900 + 1600 = c^2$$
$$2500 = c^2$$
$$\sqrt{2500} = c$$
$$50 = c$$

3. 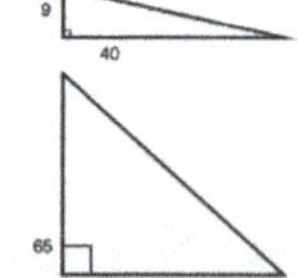

$$9^2 + 40^2 = c^2$$
$$81 + 1600 = c^2$$
$$1681 = c^2$$
$$\sqrt{1681} = c$$
$$41 = c$$

4. 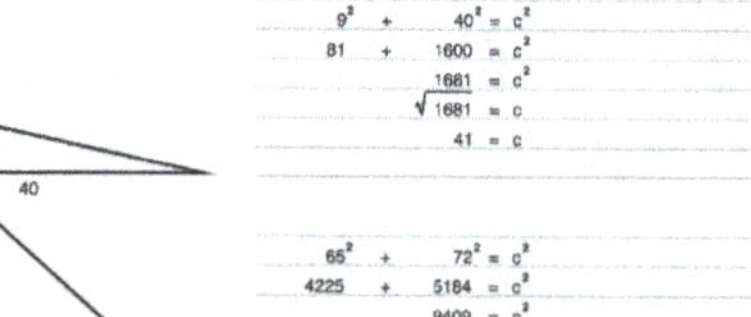

$$65^2 + 72^2 = c^2$$
$$4225 + 5184 = c^2$$
$$9409 = c^2$$
$$\sqrt{9409} = c$$
$$97 = c$$

Name:
Date: Score:

1.

$$30^2 + 40^2 = c^2$$
$$900 + 1600 = c^2$$
$$2500 = c^2$$
$$\sqrt{2500} = c$$
$$50 = c$$

2.

$$20^2 + 21^2 = c^2$$
$$400 + 441 = c^2$$
$$841 = c^2$$
$$\sqrt{841} = c$$
$$29 = c$$

3.

$$16^2 + 63^2 = c^2$$
$$256 + 3969 = c^2$$
$$4225 = c^2$$
$$\sqrt{4225} = c$$
$$65 = c$$

4.

$$3^2 + 4^2 = c^2$$
$$9 + 16 = c^2$$
$$25 = c^2$$
$$\sqrt{25} = c$$
$$5 = c$$

Name:

Date:

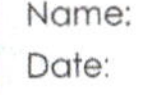

1. 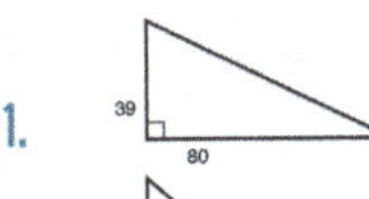

$$39^2 + 80^2 = c^2$$
$$1521 + 6400 = c^2$$
$$7921 = c^2$$
$$\sqrt{7921} = c$$
$$89 = c$$

2. 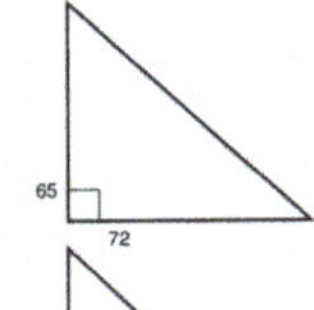

$$65^2 + 72^2 = c^2$$
$$4225 + 5184 = c^2$$
$$9409 = c^2$$
$$\sqrt{9409} = c$$
$$97 = c$$

3.

$$20^2 + 21^2 = c^2$$
$$400 + 441 = c^2$$
$$841 = c^2$$
$$\sqrt{841} = c$$
$$29 = c$$

4. 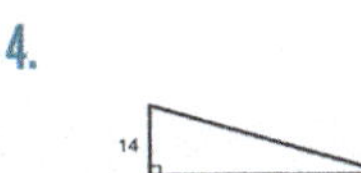

$$14^2 + 48^2 = c^2$$
$$196 + 2304 = c^2$$
$$2500 = c^2$$
$$\sqrt{2500} = c$$
$$50 = c$$

Name:

Date:

1. 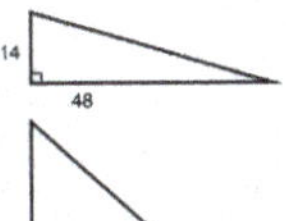

$$14^2 + 48^2 = c^2$$
$$196 + 2304 = c^2$$
$$2500 = c^2$$
$$\sqrt{2500} = c$$
$$50 = c$$

2. 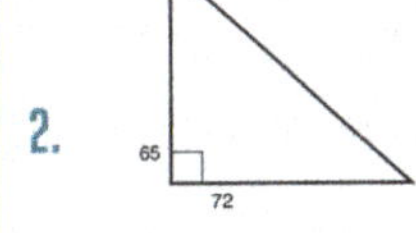

$$65^2 + 72^2 = c^2$$
$$4225 + 5184 = c^2$$
$$9409 = c^2$$
$$\sqrt{9409} = c$$
$$97 = c$$

3.

$$21^2 + 72^2 = c^2$$
$$441 + 5184 = c^2$$
$$5625 = c^2$$
$$\sqrt{5625} = c$$
$$75 = c$$

4. 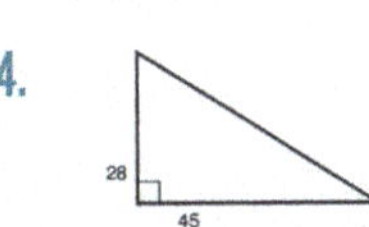

$$28^2 + 45^2 = c^2$$
$$784 + 2025 = c^2$$
$$2809 = c^2$$
$$\sqrt{2809} = c$$
$$53 = c$$

Name:

Date:

1. 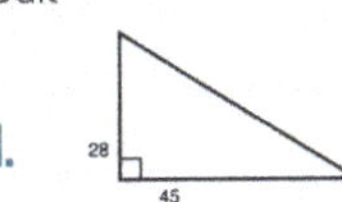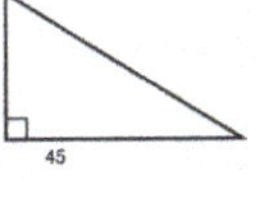

$$28^2 + 45^2 = c^2$$
$$784 + 2025 = c^2$$
$$2809 = c^2$$
$$\sqrt{2809} = c$$
$$53 = c$$

2.

$$14^2 + 48^2 = c^2$$
$$196 + 2304 = c^2$$
$$2500 = c^2$$
$$\sqrt{2500} = c$$
$$50 = c$$

3. 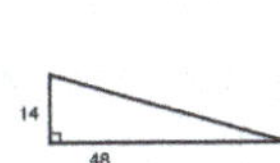

$$21^2 + 72^2 = c^2$$
$$441 + 5184 = c^2$$
$$5625 = c^2$$
$$\sqrt{5625} = c$$
$$75 = c$$

4. 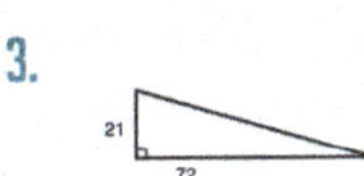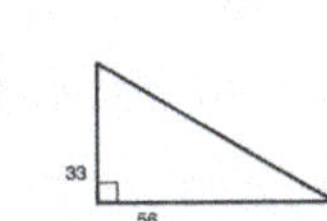

$$33^2 + 56^2 = c^2$$
$$1089 + 3136 = c^2$$
$$4225 = c^2$$
$$\sqrt{4225} = c$$
$$65 = c$$

SET 2

Find the distance between the points

Name:
Date: Score:

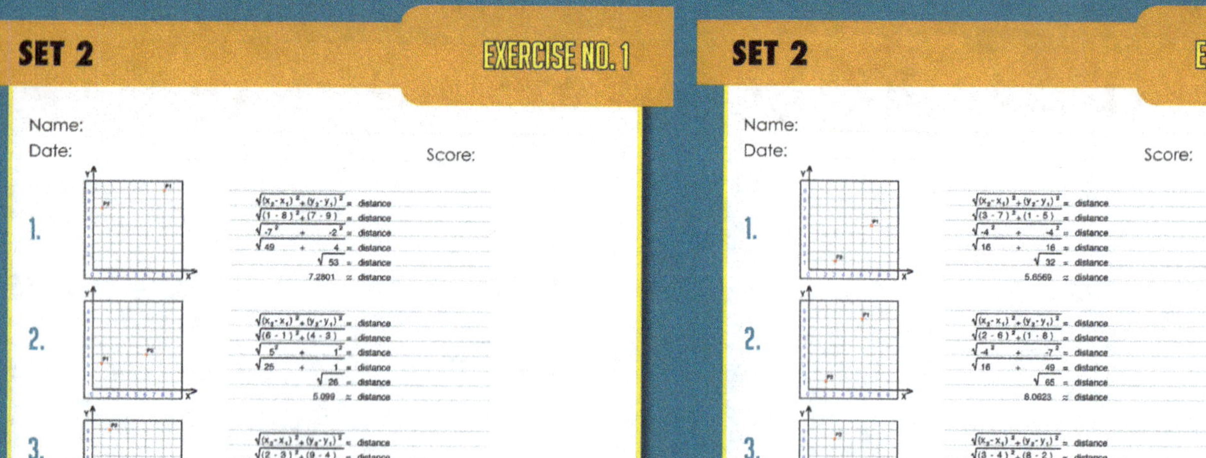

1.
$$\sqrt{(x_2 - x_1)^2 + (y_2 - y_1)^2} = \text{distance}$$
$$\sqrt{(1 - 8)^2 + (7 - 9)^2} = \text{distance}$$
$$\sqrt{-7^2 + -2^2} = \text{distance}$$
$$\sqrt{49 + 4} = \text{distance}$$
$$\sqrt{53} = \text{distance}$$
$$7.2801 \approx \text{distance}$$

2.
$$\sqrt{(x_2 - x_1)^2 + (y_2 - y_1)^2} = \text{distance}$$
$$\sqrt{(6 - 1)^2 + (4 - 3)^2} = \text{distance}$$
$$\sqrt{5^2 + 1^2} = \text{distance}$$
$$\sqrt{25 + 1} = \text{distance}$$
$$\sqrt{26} = \text{distance}$$
$$5.099 \approx \text{distance}$$

3.
$$\sqrt{(x_2 - x_1)^2 + (y_2 - y_1)^2} = \text{distance}$$
$$\sqrt{(2 - 3)^2 + (9 - 4)^2} = \text{distance}$$
$$\sqrt{-1^2 + 5^2} = \text{distance}$$
$$\sqrt{1 + 25} = \text{distance}$$
$$\sqrt{26} = \text{distance}$$
$$5.099 \approx \text{distance}$$

4.
$$\sqrt{(x_2 - x_1)^2 + (y_2 - y_1)^2} = \text{distance}$$
$$\sqrt{(6 - 5)^2 + (3 - 1)^2} = \text{distance}$$
$$\sqrt{1^2 + 2^2} = \text{distance}$$
$$\sqrt{1 + 4} = \text{distance}$$
$$\sqrt{5} = \text{distance}$$
$$2.2361 \approx \text{distance}$$

Name:
Date: Score:

1.
$$\sqrt{(x_2 - x_1)^2 + (y_2 - y_1)^2} = \text{distance}$$
$$\sqrt{(3 - 7)^2 + (1 - 5)^2} = \text{distance}$$
$$\sqrt{-4^2 + -4^2} = \text{distance}$$
$$\sqrt{16 + 16} = \text{distance}$$
$$\sqrt{32} = \text{distance}$$
$$5.6569 \approx \text{distance}$$

2.
$$\sqrt{(x_2 - x_1)^2 + (y_2 - y_1)^2} = \text{distance}$$
$$\sqrt{(2 - 6)^2 + (1 - 8)^2} = \text{distance}$$
$$\sqrt{-4^2 + -7^2} = \text{distance}$$
$$\sqrt{16 + 49} = \text{distance}$$
$$\sqrt{65} = \text{distance}$$
$$8.0623 \approx \text{distance}$$

3.
$$\sqrt{(x_2 - x_1)^2 + (y_2 - y_1)^2} = \text{distance}$$
$$\sqrt{(3 - 4)^2 + (8 - 2)^2} = \text{distance}$$
$$\sqrt{-1^2 + 6^2} = \text{distance}$$
$$\sqrt{1 + 36} = \text{distance}$$
$$\sqrt{37} = \text{distance}$$
$$6.0828 \approx \text{distance}$$

4.
$$\sqrt{(x_2 - x_1)^2 + (y_2 - y_1)^2} = \text{distance}$$
$$\sqrt{(2 - 5)^2 + (7 - 4)^2} = \text{distance}$$
$$\sqrt{-3^2 + 3^2} = \text{distance}$$
$$\sqrt{9 + 9} = \text{distance}$$
$$\sqrt{18} = \text{distance}$$
$$4.2426 \approx \text{distance}$$

Name:
Date: Score:

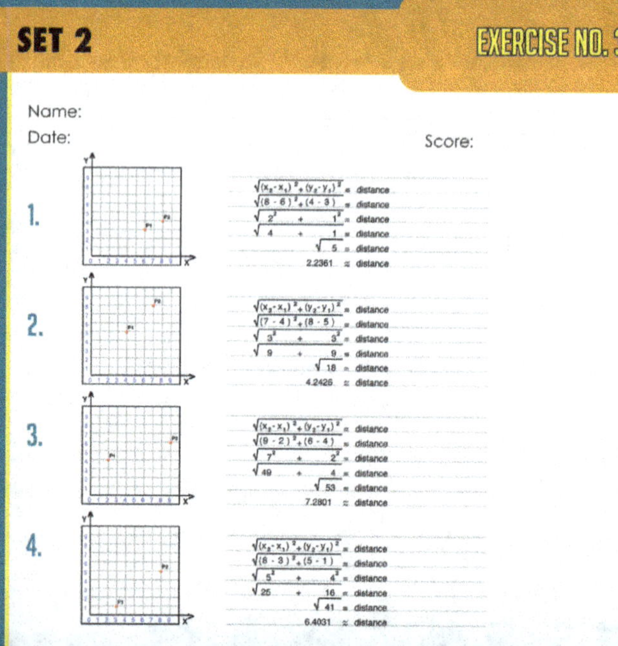

1.
$$\sqrt{(x_2 - x_1)^2 + (y_2 - y_1)^2} = \text{distance}$$
$$\sqrt{(8 - 6)^2 + (4 - 3)^2} = \text{distance}$$
$$\sqrt{2^2 + 1^2} = \text{distance}$$
$$\sqrt{4 + 1} = \text{distance}$$
$$\sqrt{5} = \text{distance}$$
$$2.2361 \approx \text{distance}$$

2.
$$\sqrt{(x_2 - x_1)^2 + (y_2 - y_1)^2} = \text{distance}$$
$$\sqrt{(7 - 4)^2 + (8 - 5)^2} = \text{distance}$$
$$\sqrt{3^2 + 3^2} = \text{distance}$$
$$\sqrt{9 + 9} = \text{distance}$$
$$\sqrt{18} = \text{distance}$$
$$4.2426 \approx \text{distance}$$

3.
$$\sqrt{(x_2 - x_1)^2 + (y_2 - y_1)^2} = \text{distance}$$
$$\sqrt{(9 - 2)^2 + (6 - 4)^2} = \text{distance}$$
$$\sqrt{7^2 + 2^2} = \text{distance}$$
$$\sqrt{49 + 4} = \text{distance}$$
$$\sqrt{53} = \text{distance}$$
$$7.2801 \approx \text{distance}$$

4.
$$\sqrt{(x_2 - x_1)^2 + (y_2 - y_1)^2} = \text{distance}$$
$$\sqrt{(8 - 3)^2 + (5 - 1)^2} = \text{distance}$$
$$\sqrt{5^2 + 4^2} = \text{distance}$$
$$\sqrt{25 + 16} = \text{distance}$$
$$\sqrt{41} = \text{distance}$$
$$6.4031 \approx \text{distance}$$

Name:
Date: Score:

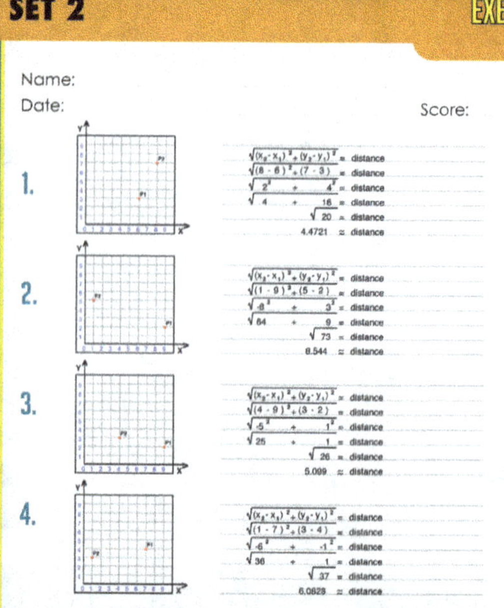

1.
$$\sqrt{(x_2 - x_1)^2 + (y_2 - y_1)^2} = \text{distance}$$
$$\sqrt{(8 - 6)^2 + (7 - 3)^2} = \text{distance}$$
$$\sqrt{2^2 + 4^2} = \text{distance}$$
$$\sqrt{4 + 16} = \text{distance}$$
$$\sqrt{20} = \text{distance}$$
$$4.4721 \approx \text{distance}$$

2.
$$\sqrt{(x_2 - x_1)^2 + (y_2 - y_1)^2} = \text{distance}$$
$$\sqrt{(1 - 9)^2 + (5 - 2)^2} = \text{distance}$$
$$\sqrt{-8^2 + 3^2} = \text{distance}$$
$$\sqrt{64 + 9} = \text{distance}$$
$$\sqrt{73} = \text{distance}$$
$$8.544 \approx \text{distance}$$

3.
$$\sqrt{(x_2 - x_1)^2 + (y_2 - y_1)^2} = \text{distance}$$
$$\sqrt{(4 - 9)^2 + (3 - 2)^2} = \text{distance}$$
$$\sqrt{-5^2 + 1^2} = \text{distance}$$
$$\sqrt{25 + 1} = \text{distance}$$
$$\sqrt{26} = \text{distance}$$
$$5.099 \approx \text{distance}$$

4.
$$\sqrt{(x_2 - x_1)^2 + (y_2 - y_1)^2} = \text{distance}$$
$$\sqrt{(1 - 7)^2 + (3 - 4)^2} = \text{distance}$$
$$\sqrt{-6^2 + -1^2} = \text{distance}$$
$$\sqrt{36 + 1} = \text{distance}$$
$$\sqrt{37} = \text{distance}$$
$$6.0828 \approx \text{distance}$$

Name:
Date: Score:

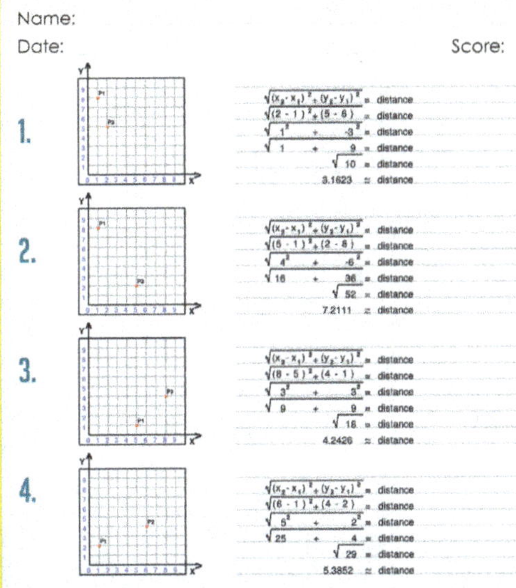

1.
$$\sqrt{(x_2-x_1)^2+(y_2-y_1)^2} = \text{distance}$$
$$\sqrt{(2-1)^2+(5-6)^2} = \text{distance}$$
$$\sqrt{1^2 + \text{-}3^2} = \text{distance}$$
$$\sqrt{1 + 9} = \text{distance}$$
$$\sqrt{10} = \text{distance}$$
$$3.1623 \approx \text{distance}$$

2.
$$\sqrt{(x_2-x_1)^2+(y_2-y_1)^2} = \text{distance}$$
$$\sqrt{(5-1)^2+(2-8)^2} = \text{distance}$$
$$\sqrt{4^2 + \text{-}6^2} = \text{distance}$$
$$\sqrt{16 + 36} = \text{distance}$$
$$\sqrt{52} = \text{distance}$$
$$7.2111 \approx \text{distance}$$

3.
$$\sqrt{(x_2-x_1)^2+(y_2-y_1)^2} = \text{distance}$$
$$\sqrt{(8-5)^2+(4-1)^2} = \text{distance}$$
$$\sqrt{3^2 + 3^2} = \text{distance}$$
$$\sqrt{9 + 9} = \text{distance}$$
$$\sqrt{18} = \text{distance}$$
$$4.2426 \approx \text{distance}$$

4.
$$\sqrt{(x_2-x_1)^2+(y_2-y_1)^2} = \text{distance}$$
$$\sqrt{(6-1)^2+(4-2)^2} = \text{distance}$$
$$\sqrt{5^2 + 2^2} = \text{distance}$$
$$\sqrt{25 + 4} = \text{distance}$$
$$\sqrt{29} = \text{distance}$$
$$5.3852 \approx \text{distance}$$

Name:
Date: Score:

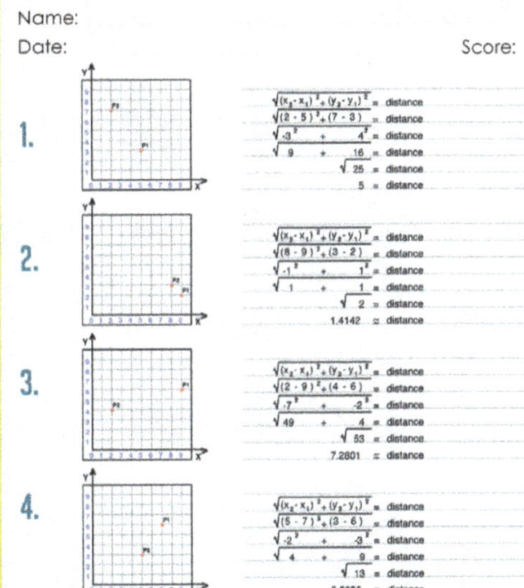

1.
$$\sqrt{(x_2-x_1)^2+(y_2-y_1)^2} = \text{distance}$$
$$\sqrt{(2-5)^2+(7-3)^2} = \text{distance}$$
$$\sqrt{\text{-}3^2 + 4^2} = \text{distance}$$
$$\sqrt{9 + 16} = \text{distance}$$
$$\sqrt{25} = \text{distance}$$
$$5 = \text{distance}$$

2.
$$\sqrt{(x_2-x_1)^2+(y_2-y_1)^2} = \text{distance}$$
$$\sqrt{(8-9)^2+(3-2)^2} = \text{distance}$$
$$\sqrt{\text{-}1^2 + 1^2} = \text{distance}$$
$$\sqrt{1 + 1} = \text{distance}$$
$$\sqrt{2} = \text{distance}$$
$$1.4142 \approx \text{distance}$$

3.
$$\sqrt{(x_2-x_1)^2+(y_2-y_1)^2} = \text{distance}$$
$$\sqrt{(2-9)^2+(4-6)^2} = \text{distance}$$
$$\sqrt{\text{-}7^2 + \text{-}2^2} = \text{distance}$$
$$\sqrt{49 + 4} = \text{distance}$$
$$\sqrt{53} = \text{distance}$$
$$7.2801 \approx \text{distance}$$

4.
$$\sqrt{(x_2-x_1)^2+(y_2-y_1)^2} = \text{distance}$$
$$\sqrt{(5-7)^2+(3-6)^2} = \text{distance}$$
$$\sqrt{\text{-}2^2 + \text{-}3^2} = \text{distance}$$
$$\sqrt{4 + 9} = \text{distance}$$
$$\sqrt{13} = \text{distance}$$
$$3.6056 \approx \text{distance}$$

Name:
Date: Score:

1.
$$\sqrt{(x_2-x_1)^2+(y_2-y_1)^2} = \text{distance}$$
$$\sqrt{(3-4)^2+(2-8)^2} = \text{distance}$$
$$\sqrt{\text{-}1^2 + \text{-}6^2} = \text{distance}$$
$$\sqrt{1 + 36} = \text{distance}$$
$$\sqrt{37} = \text{distance}$$
$$6.0828 \approx \text{distance}$$

2.
$$\sqrt{(x_2-x_1)^2+(y_2-y_1)^2} = \text{distance}$$
$$\sqrt{(6-2)^2+(7-3)^2} = \text{distance}$$
$$\sqrt{4^2 + 4^2} = \text{distance}$$
$$\sqrt{16 + 16} = \text{distance}$$
$$\sqrt{32} = \text{distance}$$
$$5.6569 \approx \text{distance}$$

3.
$$\sqrt{(x_2-x_1)^2+(y_2-y_1)^2} = \text{distance}$$
$$\sqrt{(9-1)^2+(6-3)^2} = \text{distance}$$
$$\sqrt{8^2 + 3^2} = \text{distance}$$
$$\sqrt{64 + 9} = \text{distance}$$
$$\sqrt{73} = \text{distance}$$
$$8.544 \approx \text{distance}$$

4.
$$\sqrt{(x_2-x_1)^2+(y_2-y_1)^2} = \text{distance}$$
$$\sqrt{(6-1)^2+(4-5)^2} = \text{distance}$$
$$\sqrt{7^2 + \text{-}1^2} = \text{distance}$$
$$\sqrt{49 + 1} = \text{distance}$$
$$\sqrt{50} = \text{distance}$$
$$7.0711 \approx \text{distance}$$

Name:
Date: Score:

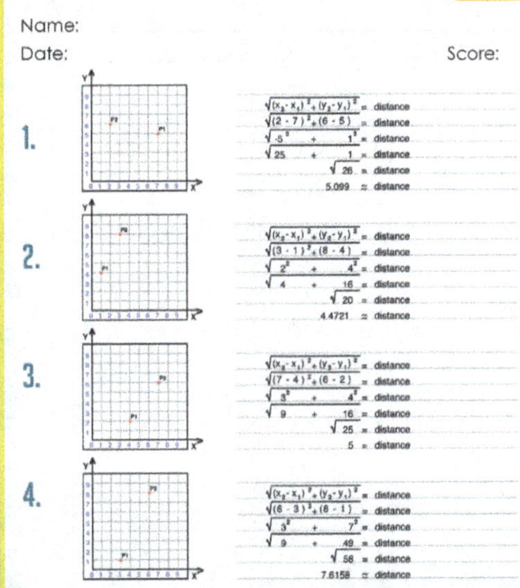

1.
$$\sqrt{(x_2-x_1)^2+(y_2-y_1)^2} = \text{distance}$$
$$\sqrt{(2-7)^2+(6-5)^2} = \text{distance}$$
$$\sqrt{\text{-}5^2 + 1^2} = \text{distance}$$
$$\sqrt{25 + 1} = \text{distance}$$
$$\sqrt{26} = \text{distance}$$
$$5.099 \approx \text{distance}$$

2.
$$\sqrt{(x_2-x_1)^2+(y_2-y_1)^2} = \text{distance}$$
$$\sqrt{(3-1)^2+(8-4)^2} = \text{distance}$$
$$\sqrt{2^2 + 4^2} = \text{distance}$$
$$\sqrt{4 + 16} = \text{distance}$$
$$\sqrt{20} = \text{distance}$$
$$4.4721 \approx \text{distance}$$

3.
$$\sqrt{(x_2-x_1)^2+(y_2-y_1)^2} = \text{distance}$$
$$\sqrt{(7-4)^2+(6-2)^2} = \text{distance}$$
$$\sqrt{3^2 + 4^2} = \text{distance}$$
$$\sqrt{9 + 16} = \text{distance}$$
$$\sqrt{25} = \text{distance}$$
$$5 = \text{distance}$$

4.
$$\sqrt{(x_2-x_1)^2+(y_2-y_1)^2} = \text{distance}$$
$$\sqrt{(6-3)^2+(8-1)^2} = \text{distance}$$
$$\sqrt{3^2 + 7^2} = \text{distance}$$
$$\sqrt{9 + 49} = \text{distance}$$
$$\sqrt{58} = \text{distance}$$
$$7.6158 \approx \text{distance}$$

Name:
Date: Score:

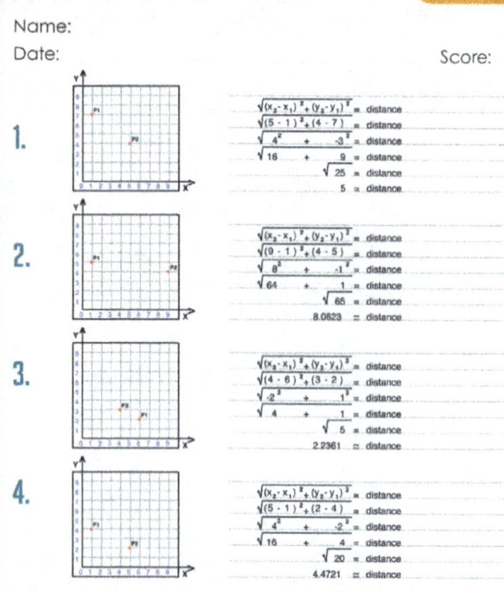

1.
$$\sqrt{(x_2-x_1)^2+(y_2-y_1)^2} = \text{distance}$$
$$\sqrt{(5-1)^2+(4-7)^2} = \text{distance}$$
$$\sqrt{4^2 + (-3)^2} = \text{distance}$$
$$\sqrt{16 + 9} = \text{distance}$$
$$\sqrt{25} = \text{distance}$$
$$5 = \text{distance}$$

2.
$$\sqrt{(x_2-x_1)^2+(y_2-y_1)^2} = \text{distance}$$
$$\sqrt{(9-1)^2+(4-5)^2} = \text{distance}$$
$$\sqrt{8^2 + (-1)^2} = \text{distance}$$
$$\sqrt{64 + 1} = \text{distance}$$
$$\sqrt{65} = \text{distance}$$
$$8.0623 \approx \text{distance}$$

3.
$$\sqrt{(x_2-x_1)^2+(y_2-y_1)^2} = \text{distance}$$
$$\sqrt{(4-6)^2+(3-2)^2} = \text{distance}$$
$$\sqrt{(-2)^2 + 1^2} = \text{distance}$$
$$\sqrt{4 + 1} = \text{distance}$$
$$\sqrt{5} = \text{distance}$$
$$2.2361 \approx \text{distance}$$

4.
$$\sqrt{(x_2-x_1)^2+(y_2-y_1)^2} = \text{distance}$$
$$\sqrt{(5-1)^2+(2-4)^2} = \text{distance}$$
$$\sqrt{4^2 + (-2)^2} = \text{distance}$$
$$\sqrt{16 + 4} = \text{distance}$$
$$\sqrt{20} = \text{distance}$$
$$4.4721 \approx \text{distance}$$

Name:
Date: Score:

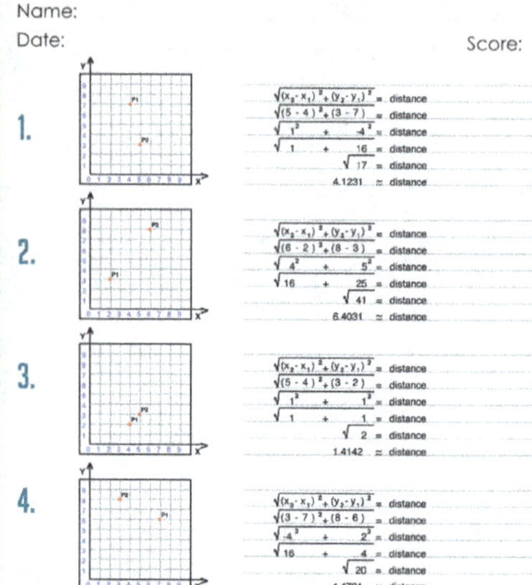

1.
$$\sqrt{(x_2-x_1)^2+(y_2-y_1)^2} = \text{distance}$$
$$\sqrt{(5-4)^2+(3-7)^2} = \text{distance}$$
$$\sqrt{1^2 + (-4)^2} = \text{distance}$$
$$\sqrt{1 + 16} = \text{distance}$$
$$\sqrt{17} = \text{distance}$$
$$4.1231 \approx \text{distance}$$

2.
$$\sqrt{(x_2-x_1)^2+(y_2-y_1)^2} = \text{distance}$$
$$\sqrt{(6-2)^2+(8-3)^2} = \text{distance}$$
$$\sqrt{4^2 + 5^2} = \text{distance}$$
$$\sqrt{16 + 25} = \text{distance}$$
$$\sqrt{41} = \text{distance}$$
$$6.4031 \approx \text{distance}$$

3.
$$\sqrt{(x_2-x_1)^2+(y_2-y_1)^2} = \text{distance}$$
$$\sqrt{(5-4)^2+(3-2)^2} = \text{distance}$$
$$\sqrt{1^2 + 1^2} = \text{distance}$$
$$\sqrt{1 + 1} = \text{distance}$$
$$\sqrt{2} = \text{distance}$$
$$1.4142 \approx \text{distance}$$

4.
$$\sqrt{(x_2-x_1)^2+(y_2-y_1)^2} = \text{distance}$$
$$\sqrt{(3-7)^2+(8-6)^2} = \text{distance}$$
$$\sqrt{(-4)^2 + 2^2} = \text{distance}$$
$$\sqrt{16 + 4} = \text{distance}$$
$$\sqrt{20} = \text{distance}$$
$$4.4721 \approx \text{distance}$$

Name:
Date: Score:

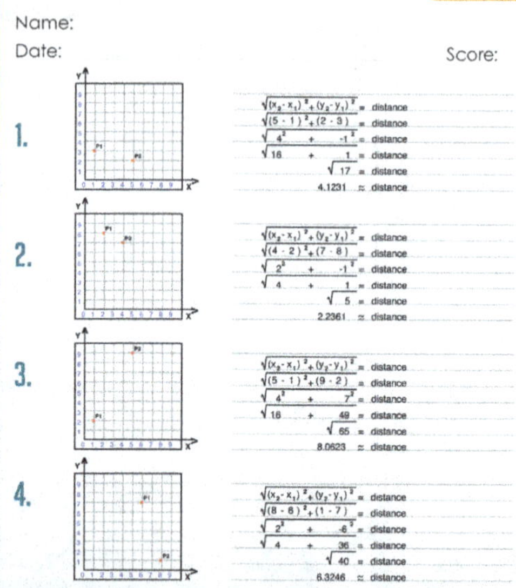

1.
$$\sqrt{(x_2-x_1)^2+(y_2-y_1)^2} = \text{distance}$$
$$\sqrt{(5-1)^2+(2-3)^2} = \text{distance}$$
$$\sqrt{4^2 + (-1)^2} = \text{distance}$$
$$\sqrt{16 + 1} = \text{distance}$$
$$\sqrt{17} = \text{distance}$$
$$4.1231 \approx \text{distance}$$

2.
$$\sqrt{(x_2-x_1)^2+(y_2-y_1)^2} = \text{distance}$$
$$\sqrt{(4-2)^2+(7-8)^2} = \text{distance}$$
$$\sqrt{2^2 + (-1)^2} = \text{distance}$$
$$\sqrt{4 + 1} = \text{distance}$$
$$\sqrt{5} = \text{distance}$$
$$2.2361 \approx \text{distance}$$

3.
$$\sqrt{(x_2-x_1)^2+(y_2-y_1)^2} = \text{distance}$$
$$\sqrt{(5-1)^2+(9-2)^2} = \text{distance}$$
$$\sqrt{4^2 + 7^2} = \text{distance}$$
$$\sqrt{16 + 49} = \text{distance}$$
$$\sqrt{65} = \text{distance}$$
$$8.0623 \approx \text{distance}$$

4.
$$\sqrt{(x_2-x_1)^2+(y_2-y_1)^2} = \text{distance}$$
$$\sqrt{(8-6)^2+(1-7)^2} = \text{distance}$$
$$\sqrt{2^2 + (-6)^2} = \text{distance}$$
$$\sqrt{4 + 36} = \text{distance}$$
$$\sqrt{40} = \text{distance}$$
$$6.3246 \approx \text{distance}$$

Name:
Date: Score:

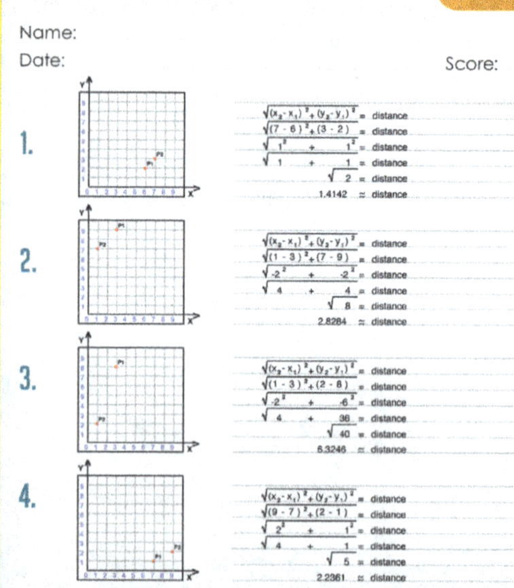

1.
$$\sqrt{(x_2-x_1)^2+(y_2-y_1)^2} = \text{distance}$$
$$\sqrt{(7-6)^2+(3-2)^2} = \text{distance}$$
$$\sqrt{1^2 + 1^2} = \text{distance}$$
$$\sqrt{1 + 1} = \text{distance}$$
$$\sqrt{2} = \text{distance}$$
$$1.4142 \approx \text{distance}$$

2.
$$\sqrt{(x_2-x_1)^2+(y_2-y_1)^2} = \text{distance}$$
$$\sqrt{(1-3)^2+(7-9)^2} = \text{distance}$$
$$\sqrt{(-2)^2 + (-2)^2} = \text{distance}$$
$$\sqrt{4 + 4} = \text{distance}$$
$$\sqrt{8} = \text{distance}$$
$$2.8284 \approx \text{distance}$$

3.
$$\sqrt{(x_2-x_1)^2+(y_2-y_1)^2} = \text{distance}$$
$$\sqrt{(1-3)^2+(2-8)^2} = \text{distance}$$
$$\sqrt{(-2)^2 + (-6)^2} = \text{distance}$$
$$\sqrt{4 + 36} = \text{distance}$$
$$\sqrt{40} = \text{distance}$$
$$6.3246 \approx \text{distance}$$

4.
$$\sqrt{(x_2-x_1)^2+(y_2-y_1)^2} = \text{distance}$$
$$\sqrt{(9-7)^2+(2-1)^2} = \text{distance}$$
$$\sqrt{2^2 + 1^2} = \text{distance}$$
$$\sqrt{4 + 1} = \text{distance}$$
$$\sqrt{5} = \text{distance}$$
$$2.2361 \approx \text{distance}$$

Name:
Date: Score:

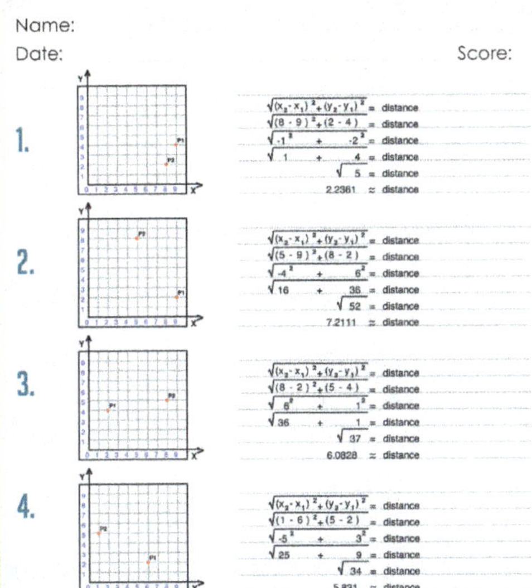

1.

$$\sqrt{(x_2 - x_1)^2 + (y_2 - y_1)^2} = \text{distance}$$
$$\sqrt{(8 - 9)^2 + (2 - 4)} = \text{distance}$$
$$\sqrt{-1^2 + -2^2} = \text{distance}$$
$$\sqrt{1 + 4} = \text{distance}$$
$$\sqrt{5} = \text{distance}$$
$$2.2361 \approx \text{distance}$$

2.

$$\sqrt{(x_2 - x_1)^2 + (y_2 - y_1)^2} = \text{distance}$$
$$\sqrt{(5 - 9)^2 + (8 - 2)} = \text{distance}$$
$$\sqrt{-4^2 + 6^2} = \text{distance}$$
$$\sqrt{16 + 36} = \text{distance}$$
$$\sqrt{52} = \text{distance}$$
$$7.2111 \approx \text{distance}$$

3.

$$\sqrt{(x_2 - x_1)^2 + (y_2 - y_1)^2} = \text{distance}$$
$$\sqrt{(8 - 2)^2 + (5 - 4)} = \text{distance}$$
$$\sqrt{6^2 + 1^2} = \text{distance}$$
$$\sqrt{36 + 1} = \text{distance}$$
$$\sqrt{37} = \text{distance}$$
$$6.0828 \approx \text{distance}$$

4.

$$\sqrt{(x_2 - x_1)^2 + (y_2 - y_1)^2} = \text{distance}$$
$$\sqrt{(1 - 6)^2 + (5 - 2)} = \text{distance}$$
$$\sqrt{-5^2 + 3^2} = \text{distance}$$
$$\sqrt{25 + 9} = \text{distance}$$
$$\sqrt{34} = \text{distance}$$
$$5.831 \approx \text{distance}$$

Name:
Date: Score:

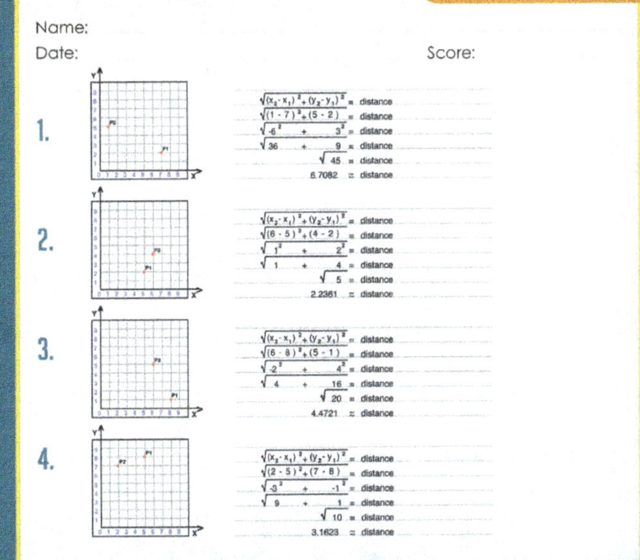

1.

$$\sqrt{(x_2 - x_1)^2 + (y_2 - y_1)^2} = \text{distance}$$
$$\sqrt{(1 - 7)^2 + (5 - 2)} = \text{distance}$$
$$\sqrt{-6^2 + 3^2} = \text{distance}$$
$$\sqrt{36 + 9} = \text{distance}$$
$$\sqrt{45} = \text{distance}$$
$$6.7082 \approx \text{distance}$$

2.

$$\sqrt{(x_2 - x_1)^2 + (y_2 - y_1)^2} = \text{distance}$$
$$\sqrt{(6 - 5)^2 + (4 - 2)} = \text{distance}$$
$$\sqrt{1^2 + -2^2} = \text{distance}$$
$$\sqrt{1 + 4} = \text{distance}$$
$$\sqrt{5} = \text{distance}$$
$$2.2361 \approx \text{distance}$$

3.

$$\sqrt{(x_2 - x_1)^2 + (y_2 - y_1)^2} = \text{distance}$$
$$\sqrt{(6 - 8)^2 + (5 - 1)} = \text{distance}$$
$$\sqrt{-2^2 + 4^2} = \text{distance}$$
$$\sqrt{4 + 16} = \text{distance}$$
$$\sqrt{20} = \text{distance}$$
$$4.4721 \approx \text{distance}$$

4.

$$\sqrt{(x_2 - x_1)^2 + (y_2 - y_1)^2} = \text{distance}$$
$$\sqrt{(2 - 5)^2 + (7 - 8)} = \text{distance}$$
$$\sqrt{-3^2 + -1^2} = \text{distance}$$
$$\sqrt{9 + 1} = \text{distance}$$
$$\sqrt{10} = \text{distance}$$
$$3.1623 \approx \text{distance}$$

Name:
Date: Score:

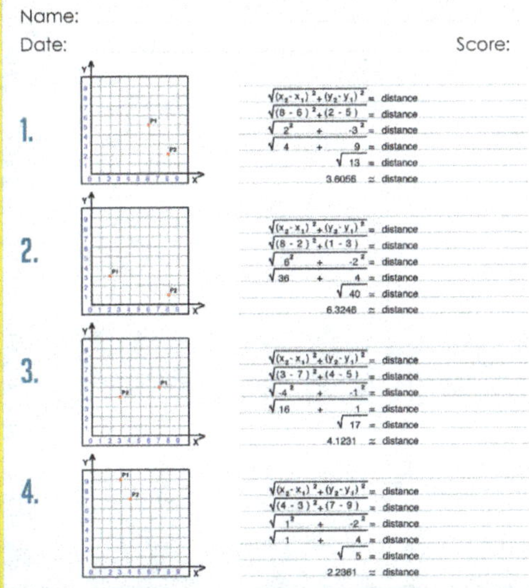

1.

$$\sqrt{(x_2 - x_1)^2 + (y_2 - y_1)^2} = \text{distance}$$
$$\sqrt{(8 - 6)^2 + (2 - 5)} = \text{distance}$$
$$\sqrt{2^2 + -3^2} = \text{distance}$$
$$\sqrt{4 + 9} = \text{distance}$$
$$\sqrt{13} = \text{distance}$$
$$3.6056 \approx \text{distance}$$

2.

$$\sqrt{(x_2 - x_1)^2 + (y_2 - y_1)^2} = \text{distance}$$
$$\sqrt{(8 - 2)^2 + (1 - 3)} = \text{distance}$$
$$\sqrt{6^2 + -2^2} = \text{distance}$$
$$\sqrt{36 + 4} = \text{distance}$$
$$\sqrt{40} = \text{distance}$$
$$6.3246 \approx \text{distance}$$

3.

$$\sqrt{(x_2 - x_1)^2 + (y_2 - y_1)^2} = \text{distance}$$
$$\sqrt{(3 - 7)^2 + (4 - 5)} = \text{distance}$$
$$\sqrt{-4^2 + -1^2} = \text{distance}$$
$$\sqrt{16 + 1} = \text{distance}$$
$$\sqrt{17} = \text{distance}$$
$$4.1231 \approx \text{distance}$$

4.

$$\sqrt{(x_2 - x_1)^2 + (y_2 - y_1)^2} = \text{distance}$$
$$\sqrt{(4 - 3)^2 + (7 - 9)} = \text{distance}$$
$$\sqrt{1^2 + -2^2} = \text{distance}$$
$$\sqrt{1 + 4} = \text{distance}$$
$$\sqrt{5} = \text{distance}$$
$$2.2361 \approx \text{distance}$$

SET 3

Find the measure of the missing angle.

Name:
Date:
Score:

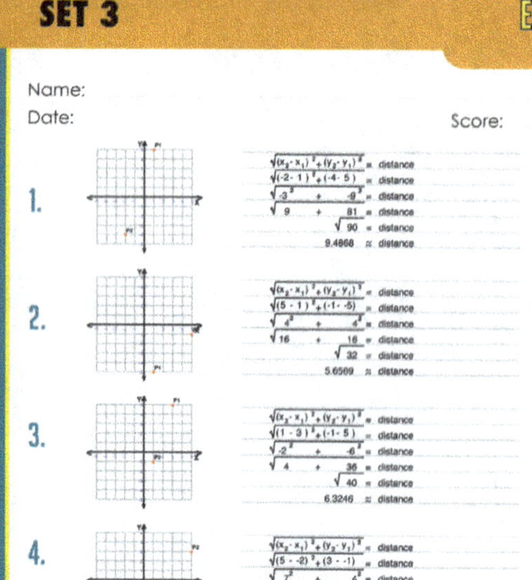

1.
$$\sqrt{(x_2-x_1)^2+(y_2-y_1)^2} = \text{distance}$$
$$\sqrt{(-2-1)^2+(-4-5)^2} = \text{distance}$$
$$\sqrt{-3^2 + -9^2} = \text{distance}$$
$$\sqrt{9 + 81} = \text{distance}$$
$$\sqrt{90} = \text{distance}$$
$$9.4868 \approx \text{distance}$$

2.
$$\sqrt{(x_2-x_1)^2+(y_2-y_1)^2} = \text{distance}$$
$$\sqrt{(5-1)^2+(-1-5)^2} = \text{distance}$$
$$\sqrt{4^2 + 4^2} = \text{distance}$$
$$\sqrt{16 + 16} = \text{distance}$$
$$\sqrt{32} = \text{distance}$$
$$5.6569 \approx \text{distance}$$

3.
$$\sqrt{(x_2-x_1)^2+(y_2-y_1)^2} = \text{distance}$$
$$\sqrt{(1-3)^2+(-1-5)^2} = \text{distance}$$
$$\sqrt{-2^2 + -6^2} = \text{distance}$$
$$\sqrt{4 + 36} = \text{distance}$$
$$\sqrt{40} = \text{distance}$$
$$6.3246 \approx \text{distance}$$

4.
$$\sqrt{(x_2-x_1)^2+(y_2-y_1)^2} = \text{distance}$$
$$\sqrt{(5-2)^2+(3-1)^2} = \text{distance}$$
$$\sqrt{7^2 + 4^2} = \text{distance}$$
$$\sqrt{49 + 16} = \text{distance}$$
$$\sqrt{65} = \text{distance}$$
$$8.0623 \approx \text{distance}$$

Name:
Date:
Score:

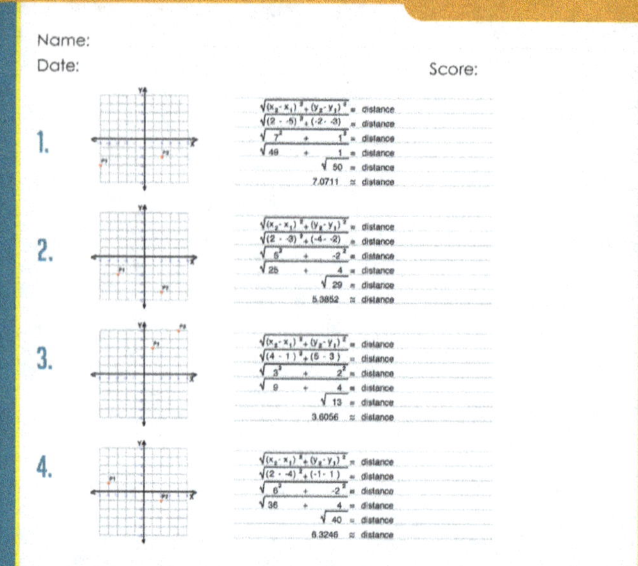

1.
$$\sqrt{(x_2-x_1)^2+(y_2-y_1)^2} = \text{distance}$$
$$\sqrt{(2-5)^2+(-2-3)^2} = \text{distance}$$
$$\sqrt{7^2 + 1^2} = \text{distance}$$
$$\sqrt{49 + 1} = \text{distance}$$
$$\sqrt{50} = \text{distance}$$
$$7.0711 \approx \text{distance}$$

2.
$$\sqrt{(x_2-x_1)^2+(y_2-y_1)^2} = \text{distance}$$
$$\sqrt{(2-3)^2+(-4-2)^2} = \text{distance}$$
$$\sqrt{5^2 + -2^2} = \text{distance}$$
$$\sqrt{25 + 4} = \text{distance}$$
$$\sqrt{29} = \text{distance}$$
$$5.3852 \approx \text{distance}$$

3.
$$\sqrt{(x_2-x_1)^2+(y_2-y_1)^2} = \text{distance}$$
$$\sqrt{(4-1)^2+(5-3)^2} = \text{distance}$$
$$\sqrt{3^2 + 2^2} = \text{distance}$$
$$\sqrt{9 + 4} = \text{distance}$$
$$\sqrt{13} = \text{distance}$$
$$3.6056 \approx \text{distance}$$

4.
$$\sqrt{(x_2-x_1)^2+(y_2-y_1)^2} = \text{distance}$$
$$\sqrt{(2-4)^2+(-1-1)^2} = \text{distance}$$
$$\sqrt{6^2 + -2^2} = \text{distance}$$
$$\sqrt{36 + 4} = \text{distance}$$
$$\sqrt{40} = \text{distance}$$
$$6.3246 \approx \text{distance}$$

Name:
Date:
Score:

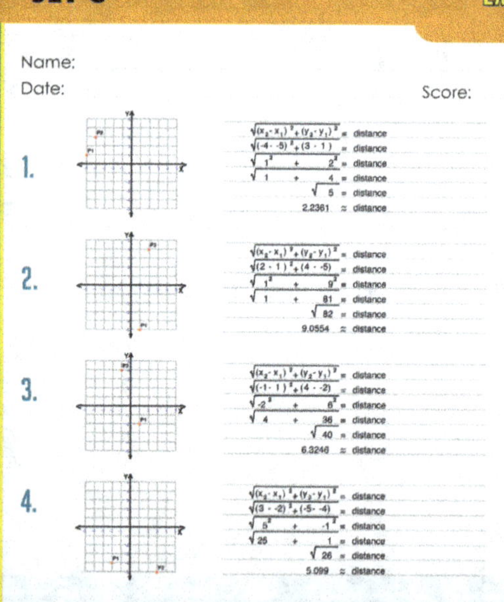

1.
$$\sqrt{(x_2-x_1)^2+(y_2-y_1)^2} = \text{distance}$$
$$\sqrt{(-4-5)^2+(3-1)^2} = \text{distance}$$
$$\sqrt{1^2 + 2^2} = \text{distance}$$
$$\sqrt{1 + 4} = \text{distance}$$
$$\sqrt{5} = \text{distance}$$
$$2.2361 \approx \text{distance}$$

2.
$$\sqrt{(x_2-x_1)^2+(y_2-y_1)^2} = \text{distance}$$
$$\sqrt{(2-1)^2+(4-5)^2} = \text{distance}$$
$$\sqrt{1^2 + 9^2} = \text{distance}$$
$$\sqrt{1 + 81} = \text{distance}$$
$$\sqrt{82} = \text{distance}$$
$$9.0554 \approx \text{distance}$$

3.
$$\sqrt{(x_2-x_1)^2+(y_2-y_1)^2} = \text{distance}$$
$$\sqrt{(-1-1)^2+(4-2)^2} = \text{distance}$$
$$\sqrt{-2^2 + 6^2} = \text{distance}$$
$$\sqrt{4 + 36} = \text{distance}$$
$$\sqrt{40} = \text{distance}$$
$$6.3246 \approx \text{distance}$$

4.
$$\sqrt{(x_2-x_1)^2+(y_2-y_1)^2} = \text{distance}$$
$$\sqrt{(3-2)^2+(-5-4)^2} = \text{distance}$$
$$\sqrt{5^2 + -1^2} = \text{distance}$$
$$\sqrt{25 + 1} = \text{distance}$$
$$\sqrt{26} = \text{distance}$$
$$5.099 \approx \text{distance}$$

Name:
Date:
Score:

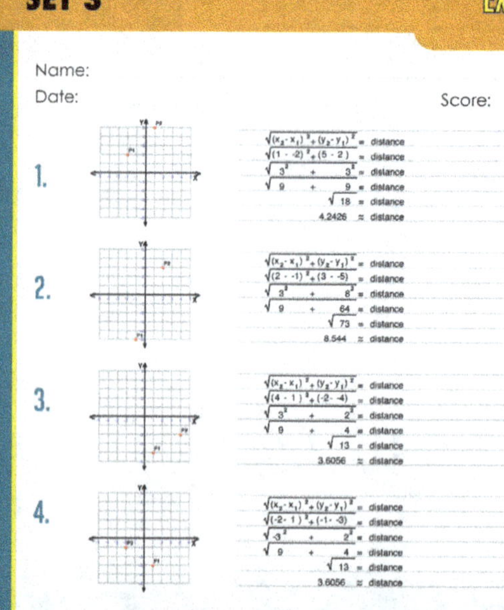

1.
$$\sqrt{(x_2-x_1)^2+(y_2-y_1)^2} = \text{distance}$$
$$\sqrt{(1-2)^2+(5-2)^2} = \text{distance}$$
$$\sqrt{3^2 + 3^2} = \text{distance}$$
$$\sqrt{9 + 9} = \text{distance}$$
$$\sqrt{18} = \text{distance}$$
$$4.2426 \approx \text{distance}$$

2.
$$\sqrt{(x_2-x_1)^2+(y_2-y_1)^2} = \text{distance}$$
$$\sqrt{(2-1)^2+(3-5)^2} = \text{distance}$$
$$\sqrt{3^2 + 8^2} = \text{distance}$$
$$\sqrt{9 + 64} = \text{distance}$$
$$\sqrt{73} = \text{distance}$$
$$8.544 \approx \text{distance}$$

3.
$$\sqrt{(x_2-x_1)^2+(y_2-y_1)^2} = \text{distance}$$
$$\sqrt{(4-1)^2+(-2-4)^2} = \text{distance}$$
$$\sqrt{3^2 + 2^2} = \text{distance}$$
$$\sqrt{9 + 4} = \text{distance}$$
$$\sqrt{13} = \text{distance}$$
$$3.6056 \approx \text{distance}$$

4.
$$\sqrt{(x_2-x_1)^2+(y_2-y_1)^2} = \text{distance}$$
$$\sqrt{(-2-1)^2+(-1-3)^2} = \text{distance}$$
$$\sqrt{-3^2 + 2^2} = \text{distance}$$
$$\sqrt{9 + 4} = \text{distance}$$
$$\sqrt{13} = \text{distance}$$
$$3.6056 \approx \text{distance}$$

Name:
Date: Score:

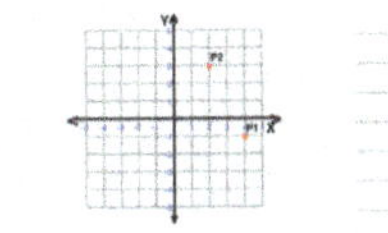

1.
$$\sqrt{(x_2 - x_1)^2 + (y_2 - y_1)^2} = \text{distance}$$
$$\sqrt{(2 - 4)^2 + (3 - -1)^2} = \text{distance}$$
$$\sqrt{-2^2 + 4^2} = \text{distance}$$
$$\sqrt{4 + 16} = \text{distance}$$
$$\sqrt{20} = \text{distance}$$
$$4.4721 \approx \text{distance}$$

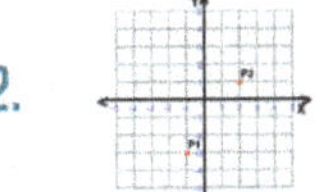

2.
$$\sqrt{(x_2 - x_1)^2 + (y_2 - y_1)^2} = \text{distance}$$
$$\sqrt{(2 - -1)^2 + (1 - -3)^2} = \text{distance}$$
$$\sqrt{3^2 + 4^2} = \text{distance}$$
$$\sqrt{9 + 16} = \text{distance}$$
$$\sqrt{25} = \text{distance}$$
$$5 = \text{distance}$$

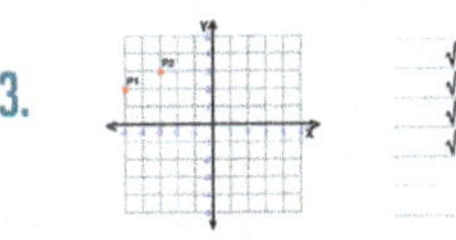

3.
$$\sqrt{(x_2 - x_1)^2 + (y_2 - y_1)^2} = \text{distance}$$
$$\sqrt{(-3 - -5)^2 + (3 - 2)^2} = \text{distance}$$
$$\sqrt{2^2 + 1^2} = \text{distance}$$
$$\sqrt{4 + 1} = \text{distance}$$
$$\sqrt{5} = \text{distance}$$
$$2.2361 \approx \text{distance}$$

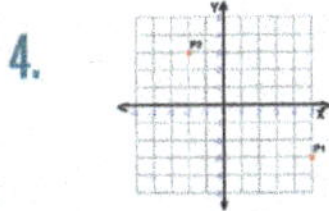
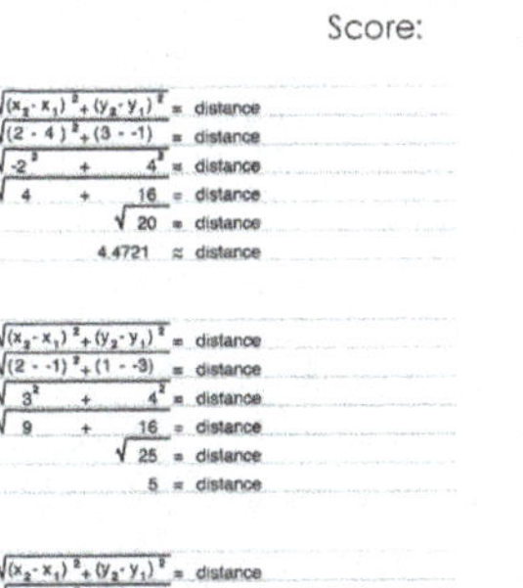
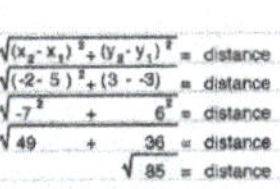

4.
$$\sqrt{(x_2 - x_1)^2 + (y_2 - y_1)^2} = \text{distance}$$
$$\sqrt{(2 - 5)^2 + (3 - -3)^2} = \text{distance}$$
$$\sqrt{-7^2 + 6^2} = \text{distance}$$
$$\sqrt{49 + 36} = \text{distance}$$
$$\sqrt{85} = \text{distance}$$
$$9.2195 \approx \text{distance}$$

Name:
Date: Score:

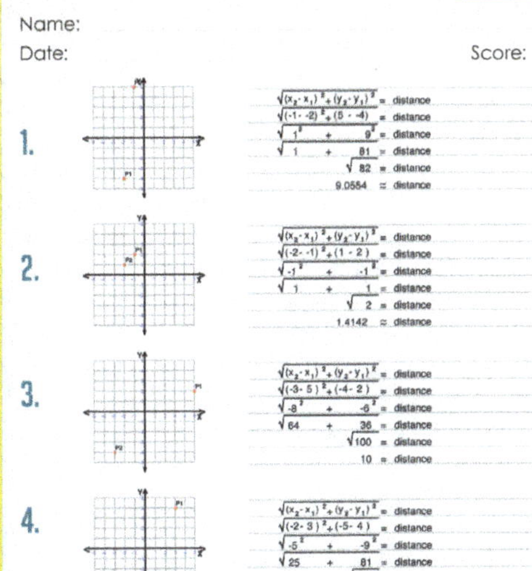

1.
$$\sqrt{(x_2 - x_1)^2 + (y_2 - y_1)^2} = \text{distance}$$
$$\sqrt{(-1 - -2)^2 + (5 - -4)^2} = \text{distance}$$
$$\sqrt{1^2 + 9^2} = \text{distance}$$
$$\sqrt{1 + 81} = \text{distance}$$
$$\sqrt{82} = \text{distance}$$
$$9.0554 \approx \text{distance}$$

2.
$$\sqrt{(x_2 - x_1)^2 + (y_2 - y_1)^2} = \text{distance}$$
$$\sqrt{(-2 - -1)^2 + (1 - 2)^2} = \text{distance}$$
$$\sqrt{-1^2 + -1^2} = \text{distance}$$
$$\sqrt{1 + 1} = \text{distance}$$
$$\sqrt{2} = \text{distance}$$
$$1.4142 \approx \text{distance}$$

3.
$$\sqrt{(x_2 - x_1)^2 + (y_2 - y_1)^2} = \text{distance}$$
$$\sqrt{(-3 - 5)^2 + (-4 - 2)^2} = \text{distance}$$
$$\sqrt{-8^2 + -6^2} = \text{distance}$$
$$\sqrt{64 + 36} = \text{distance}$$
$$\sqrt{100} = \text{distance}$$
$$10 = \text{distance}$$

4.
$$\sqrt{(x_2 - x_1)^2 + (y_2 - y_1)^2} = \text{distance}$$
$$\sqrt{(-2 - 3)^2 + (-5 - 4)^2} = \text{distance}$$
$$\sqrt{-5^2 + -9^2} = \text{distance}$$
$$\sqrt{25 + 81} = \text{distance}$$
$$\sqrt{106} = \text{distance}$$
$$10.2956 \approx \text{distance}$$

Name:
Date: Score:

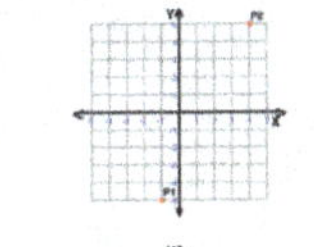

1.
$$\sqrt{(x_2 - x_1)^2 + (y_2 - y_1)^2} = \text{distance}$$
$$\sqrt{(4 - -1)^2 + (5 - -5)^2} = \text{distance}$$
$$\sqrt{5^2 + 10^2} = \text{distance}$$
$$\sqrt{25 + 100} = \text{distance}$$
$$\sqrt{125} = \text{distance}$$
$$11.1803 \approx \text{distance}$$

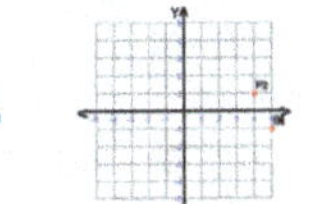

2.
$$\sqrt{(x_2 - x_1)^2 + (y_2 - y_1)^2} = \text{distance}$$
$$\sqrt{(4 - 5)^2 + (1 - -1)^2} = \text{distance}$$
$$\sqrt{-1^2 + 2^2} = \text{distance}$$
$$\sqrt{1 + 4} = \text{distance}$$
$$\sqrt{5} = \text{distance}$$
$$2.2361 \approx \text{distance}$$

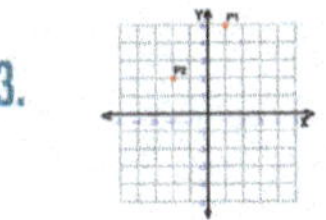
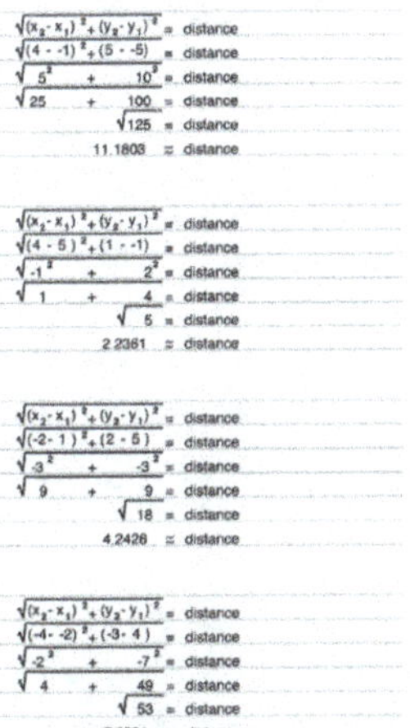

3.
$$\sqrt{(x_2 - x_1)^2 + (y_2 - y_1)^2} = \text{distance}$$
$$\sqrt{(-2 - 1)^2 + (2 - 5)^2} = \text{distance}$$
$$\sqrt{-3^2 + -3^2} = \text{distance}$$
$$\sqrt{9 + 9} = \text{distance}$$
$$\sqrt{18} = \text{distance}$$
$$4.2426 \approx \text{distance}$$

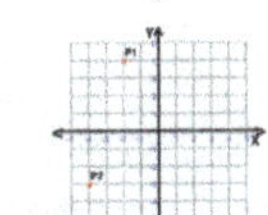

4.
$$\sqrt{(x_2 - x_1)^2 + (y_2 - y_1)^2} = \text{distance}$$
$$\sqrt{(-4 - -2)^2 + (-3 - 4)^2} = \text{distance}$$
$$\sqrt{-2^2 + -7^2} = \text{distance}$$
$$\sqrt{4 + 49} = \text{distance}$$
$$\sqrt{53} = \text{distance}$$
$$7.2801 \approx \text{distance}$$

Name:
Date: Score:

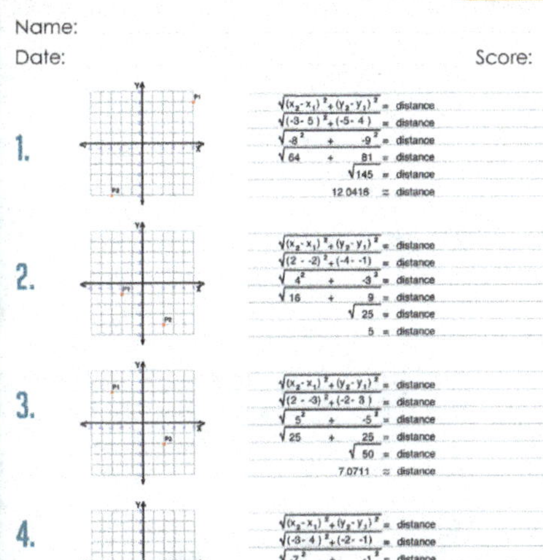

1.
$$\sqrt{(x_2 - x_1)^2 + (y_2 - y_1)^2} = \text{distance}$$
$$\sqrt{(-3 - 5)^2 + (-5 - 4)^2} = \text{distance}$$
$$\sqrt{-8^2 + -9^2} = \text{distance}$$
$$\sqrt{64 + 81} = \text{distance}$$
$$\sqrt{145} = \text{distance}$$
$$12.0416 \approx \text{distance}$$

2.
$$\sqrt{(x_2 - x_1)^2 + (y_2 - y_1)^2} = \text{distance}$$
$$\sqrt{(2 - -2)^2 + (-4 - -1)^2} = \text{distance}$$
$$\sqrt{4^2 + -3^2} = \text{distance}$$
$$\sqrt{16 + 9} = \text{distance}$$
$$\sqrt{25} = \text{distance}$$
$$5 = \text{distance}$$

3.
$$\sqrt{(x_2 - x_1)^2 + (y_2 - y_1)^2} = \text{distance}$$
$$\sqrt{(2 - -3)^2 + (-2 - 3)^2} = \text{distance}$$
$$\sqrt{5^2 + -5^2} = \text{distance}$$
$$\sqrt{25 + 25} = \text{distance}$$
$$\sqrt{50} = \text{distance}$$
$$7.0711 \approx \text{distance}$$

4.
$$\sqrt{(x_2 - x_1)^2 + (y_2 - y_1)^2} = \text{distance}$$
$$\sqrt{(-3 - 4)^2 + (-2 - -1)^2} = \text{distance}$$
$$\sqrt{-7^2 + -1^2} = \text{distance}$$
$$\sqrt{49 + 1} = \text{distance}$$
$$\sqrt{50} = \text{distance}$$
$$7.0711 \approx \text{distance}$$

Name:
Date: Score:

1. 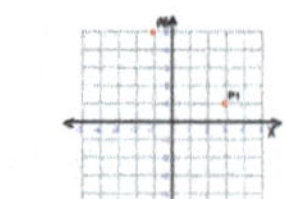 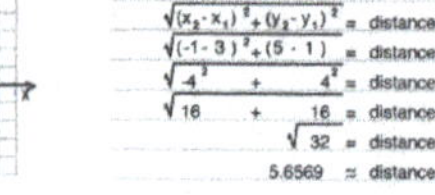

$$\sqrt{(x_2-x_1)^2+(y_2-y_1)^2} = \text{distance}$$
$$\sqrt{(-1-3)^2+(5-1)^2} = \text{distance}$$
$$\sqrt{-4^2 + 4^2} = \text{distance}$$
$$\sqrt{16 + 16} = \text{distance}$$
$$\sqrt{32} = \text{distance}$$
$$5.6569 \approx \text{distance}$$

2.  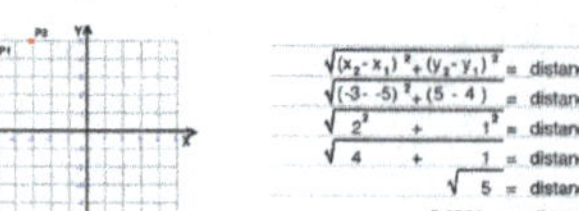

$$\sqrt{(x_2-x_1)^2+(y_2-y_1)^2} = \text{distance}$$
$$\sqrt{(-2-4)^2+(-5-2)^2} = \text{distance}$$
$$\sqrt{-6^2 + -7^2} = \text{distance}$$
$$\sqrt{36 + 49} = \text{distance}$$
$$\sqrt{85} = \text{distance}$$
$$9.2195 \approx \text{distance}$$

3. 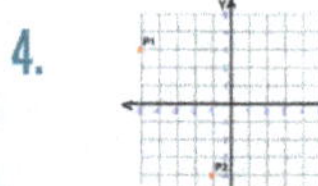

$$\sqrt{(x_2-x_1)^2+(y_2-y_1)^2} = \text{distance}$$
$$\sqrt{(-3--5)^2+(5-4)^2} = \text{distance}$$
$$\sqrt{2^2 + 1^2} = \text{distance}$$
$$\sqrt{4 + 1} = \text{distance}$$
$$\sqrt{5} = \text{distance}$$
$$2.2361 \approx \text{distance}$$

4. 

$$\sqrt{(x_2-x_1)^2+(y_2-y_1)^2} = \text{distance}$$
$$\sqrt{(-1--5)^2+(-4-3)^2} = \text{distance}$$
$$\sqrt{4^2 + -7^2} = \text{distance}$$
$$\sqrt{16 + 49} = \text{distance}$$
$$\sqrt{65} = \text{distance}$$
$$8.0623 \approx \text{distance}$$

Name:
Date: Score:

1. 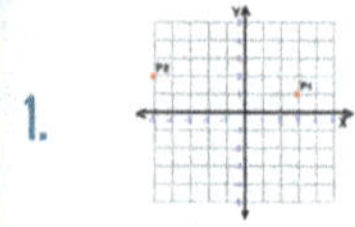 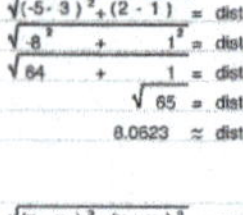

$$\sqrt{(x_2-x_1)^2+(y_2-y_1)^2} = \text{distance}$$
$$\sqrt{(-5-3)^2+(2-1)^2} = \text{distance}$$
$$\sqrt{-8^2 + 1^2} = \text{distance}$$
$$\sqrt{64 + 1} = \text{distance}$$
$$\sqrt{65} = \text{distance}$$
$$8.0623 \approx \text{distance}$$

2. 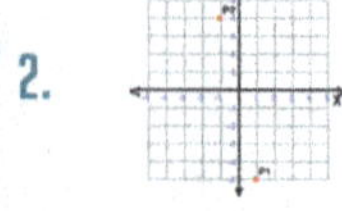

$$\sqrt{(x_2-x_1)^2+(y_2-y_1)^2} = \text{distance}$$
$$\sqrt{(-1-1)^2+(4--5)^2} = \text{distance}$$
$$\sqrt{-2^2 + 9^2} = \text{distance}$$
$$\sqrt{4 + 81} = \text{distance}$$
$$\sqrt{85} = \text{distance}$$
$$9.2195 \approx \text{distance}$$

3. 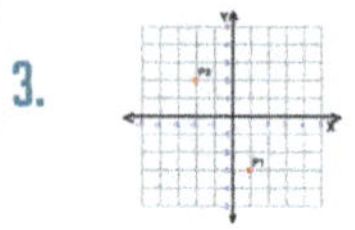

$$\sqrt{(x_2-x_1)^2+(y_2-y_1)^2} = \text{distance}$$
$$\sqrt{(-2-1)^2+(2--3)^2} = \text{distance}$$
$$\sqrt{-3^2 + 5^2} = \text{distance}$$
$$\sqrt{9 + 25} = \text{distance}$$
$$\sqrt{34} = \text{distance}$$
$$5.831 \approx \text{distance}$$

4. 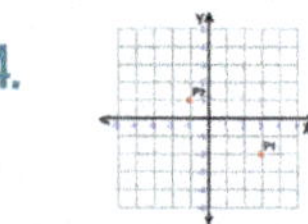

$$\sqrt{(x_2-x_1)^2+(y_2-y_1)^2} = \text{distance}$$
$$\sqrt{(-1-3)^2+(1--2)^2} = \text{distance}$$
$$\sqrt{-4^2 + 3^2} = \text{distance}$$
$$\sqrt{16 + 9} = \text{distance}$$
$$\sqrt{25} = \text{distance}$$
$$5 = \text{distance}$$

Name:
Date: Score:

1. 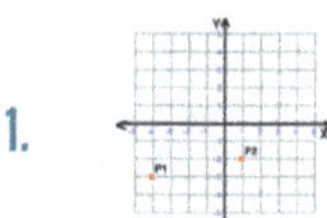 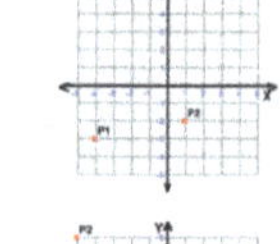 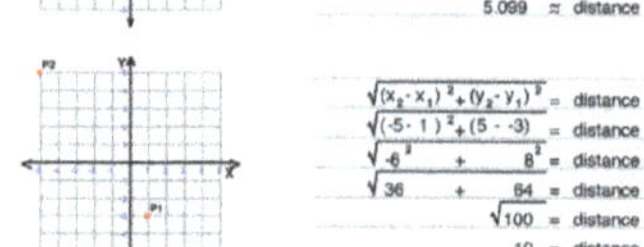

$$\sqrt{(x_2-x_1)^2+(y_2-y_1)^2} = \text{distance}$$
$$\sqrt{(1-4)^2+(-2--3)^2} = \text{distance}$$
$$\sqrt{5^2 + 1^2} = \text{distance}$$
$$\sqrt{25 + 1} = \text{distance}$$
$$\sqrt{26} = \text{distance}$$
$$5.099 \approx \text{distance}$$

2.

$$\sqrt{(x_2-x_1)^2+(y_2-y_1)^2} = \text{distance}$$
$$\sqrt{(-5-1)^2+(5--3)^2} = \text{distance}$$
$$\sqrt{-6^2 + 8^2} = \text{distance}$$
$$\sqrt{36 + 64} = \text{distance}$$
$$\sqrt{100} = \text{distance}$$
$$10 = \text{distance}$$

3.

$$\sqrt{(x_2-x_1)^2+(y_2-y_1)^2} = \text{distance}$$
$$\sqrt{(2-5)^2+(1--3)^2} = \text{distance}$$
$$\sqrt{-3^2 + 4^2} = \text{distance}$$
$$\sqrt{9 + 16} = \text{distance}$$
$$\sqrt{25} = \text{distance}$$
$$5 = \text{distance}$$

4. 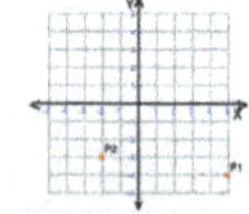

$$\sqrt{(x_2-x_1)^2+(y_2-y_1)^2} = \text{distance}$$
$$\sqrt{(-2-5)^2+(-3--4)^2} = \text{distance}$$
$$\sqrt{-7^2 + 1^2} = \text{distance}$$
$$\sqrt{49 + 1} = \text{distance}$$
$$\sqrt{50} = \text{distance}$$
$$7.0711 \approx \text{distance}$$

Name:
Date: Score:

1.

$$\sqrt{(x_2-x_1)^2+(y_2-y_1)^2} = \text{distance}$$
$$\sqrt{(-5-3)^2+(-2--1)^2} = \text{distance}$$
$$\sqrt{-8^2 + -1^2} = \text{distance}$$
$$\sqrt{64 + 1} = \text{distance}$$
$$\sqrt{65} = \text{distance}$$
$$8.0623 \approx \text{distance}$$

2. 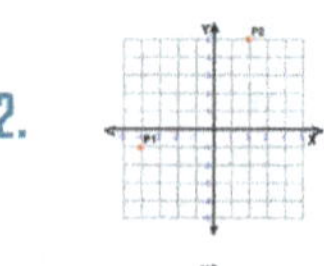 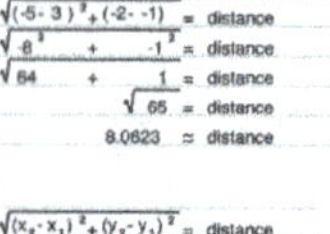  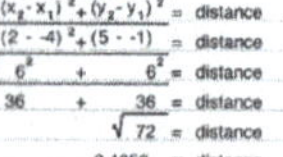

$$\sqrt{(x_2-x_1)^2+(y_2-y_1)^2} = \text{distance}$$
$$\sqrt{(2-4)^2+(5--1)^2} = \text{distance}$$
$$\sqrt{-6^2 + 6^2} = \text{distance}$$
$$\sqrt{36 + 36} = \text{distance}$$
$$\sqrt{72} = \text{distance}$$
$$8.4853 \approx \text{distance}$$

3. 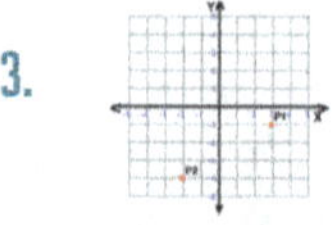 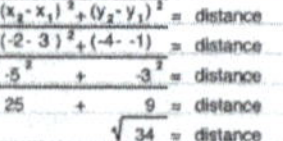

$$\sqrt{(x_2-x_1)^2+(y_2-y_1)^2} = \text{distance}$$
$$\sqrt{(-2-3)^2+(-4--1)^2} = \text{distance}$$
$$\sqrt{-5^2 + -3^2} = \text{distance}$$
$$\sqrt{25 + 9} = \text{distance}$$
$$\sqrt{34} = \text{distance}$$
$$5.831 \approx \text{distance}$$

4.  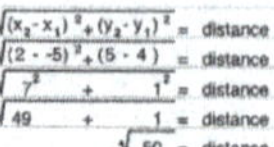

$$\sqrt{(x_2-x_1)^2+(y_2-y_1)^2} = \text{distance}$$
$$\sqrt{(2--5)^2+(5-4)^2} = \text{distance}$$
$$\sqrt{7^2 + 1^2} = \text{distance}$$
$$\sqrt{49 + 1} = \text{distance}$$
$$\sqrt{50} = \text{distance}$$
$$7.0711 \approx \text{distance}$$

Name:

Date: Score:

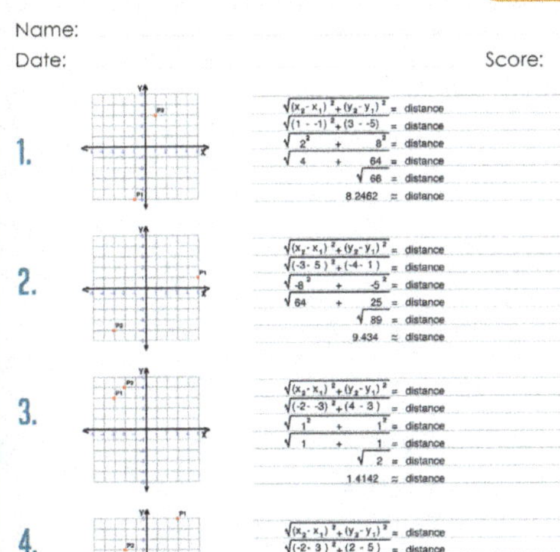

1.
$$\sqrt{(x_2 - x_1)^2 + (y_2 - y_1)^2} = \text{distance}$$
$$\sqrt{(1 - -1)^2 + (3 - -5)} = \text{distance}$$
$$\sqrt{2^2 + 8^2} = \text{distance}$$
$$\sqrt{4 + 64} = \text{distance}$$
$$\sqrt{68} = \text{distance}$$
$$8.2462 \approx \text{distance}$$

2.
$$\sqrt{(x_2 - x_1)^2 + (y_2 - y_1)^2} = \text{distance}$$
$$\sqrt{(-3 - 5)^2 + (-4 - 1)} = \text{distance}$$
$$\sqrt{-8^2 + -5^2} = \text{distance}$$
$$\sqrt{64 + 25} = \text{distance}$$
$$\sqrt{89} = \text{distance}$$
$$9.434 \approx \text{distance}$$

3.
$$\sqrt{(x_2 - x_1)^2 + (y_2 - y_1)^2} = \text{distance}$$
$$\sqrt{(-2 - -3)^2 + (4 - 3)} = \text{distance}$$
$$\sqrt{1^2 + 1^2} = \text{distance}$$
$$\sqrt{1 + 1} = \text{distance}$$
$$\sqrt{2} = \text{distance}$$
$$1.4142 \approx \text{distance}$$

4.
$$\sqrt{(x_2 - x_1)^2 + (y_2 - y_1)^2} = \text{distance}$$
$$\sqrt{(-2 - 3)^2 + (2 - 5)} = \text{distance}$$
$$\sqrt{-5^2 + -3^2} = \text{distance}$$
$$\sqrt{25 + 9} = \text{distance}$$
$$\sqrt{34} = \text{distance}$$
$$5.831 \approx \text{distance}$$

Name:

Date: Score:

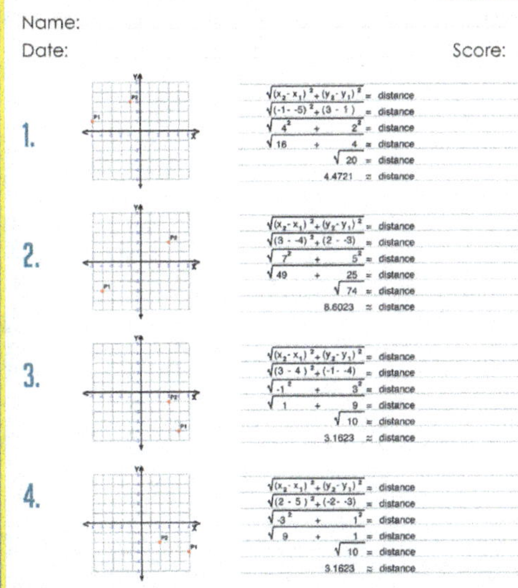

1.
$$\sqrt{(x_2 - x_1)^2 + (y_2 - y_1)^2} = \text{distance}$$
$$\sqrt{(-1 - -5)^2 + (3 - 1)} = \text{distance}$$
$$\sqrt{4^2 + 2^2} = \text{distance}$$
$$\sqrt{16 + 4} = \text{distance}$$
$$\sqrt{20} = \text{distance}$$
$$4.4721 \approx \text{distance}$$

2.
$$\sqrt{(x_2 - x_1)^2 + (y_2 - y_1)^2} = \text{distance}$$
$$\sqrt{(3 - -4)^2 + (2 - -3)} = \text{distance}$$
$$\sqrt{7^2 + 5^2} = \text{distance}$$
$$\sqrt{49 + 25} = \text{distance}$$
$$\sqrt{74} = \text{distance}$$
$$8.6023 \approx \text{distance}$$

3.
$$\sqrt{(x_2 - x_1)^2 + (y_2 - y_1)^2} = \text{distance}$$
$$\sqrt{(3 - 4)^2 + (-1 - -4)} = \text{distance}$$
$$\sqrt{-1^2 + 3^2} = \text{distance}$$
$$\sqrt{1 + 9} = \text{distance}$$
$$\sqrt{10} = \text{distance}$$
$$3.1623 \approx \text{distance}$$

4.
$$\sqrt{(x_2 - x_1)^2 + (y_2 - y_1)^2} = \text{distance}$$
$$\sqrt{(2 - 5)^2 + (-2 - -3)} = \text{distance}$$
$$\sqrt{-3^2 + 1^2} = \text{distance}$$
$$\sqrt{9 + 1} = \text{distance}$$
$$\sqrt{10} = \text{distance}$$
$$3.1623 \approx \text{distance}$$

Name:

Date: Score:

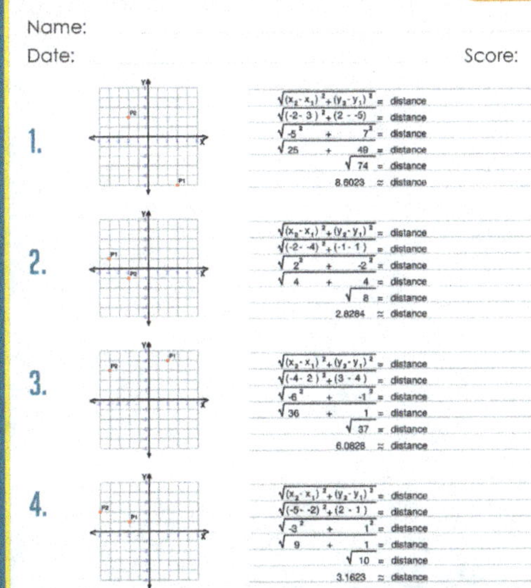

1.
$$\sqrt{(x_2 - x_1)^2 + (y_2 - y_1)^2} = \text{distance}$$
$$\sqrt{(-2 - 3)^2 + (2 - -5)} = \text{distance}$$
$$\sqrt{-5^2 + 7^2} = \text{distance}$$
$$\sqrt{25 + 49} = \text{distance}$$
$$\sqrt{74} = \text{distance}$$
$$8.6023 \approx \text{distance}$$

2.
$$\sqrt{(x_2 - x_1)^2 + (y_2 - y_1)^2} = \text{distance}$$
$$\sqrt{(-2 - -4)^2 + (-1 - 1)} = \text{distance}$$
$$\sqrt{2^2 + -2^2} = \text{distance}$$
$$\sqrt{4 + 4} = \text{distance}$$
$$\sqrt{8} = \text{distance}$$
$$2.8284 \approx \text{distance}$$

3.
$$\sqrt{(x_2 - x_1)^2 + (y_2 - y_1)^2} = \text{distance}$$
$$\sqrt{(-4 - 2)^2 + (3 - 4)} = \text{distance}$$
$$\sqrt{-6^2 + -1^2} = \text{distance}$$
$$\sqrt{36 + 1} = \text{distance}$$
$$\sqrt{37} = \text{distance}$$
$$6.0828 \approx \text{distance}$$

4.
$$\sqrt{(x_2 - x_1)^2 + (y_2 - y_1)^2} = \text{distance}$$
$$\sqrt{(-5 - -2)^2 + (2 - 1)} = \text{distance}$$
$$\sqrt{-3^2 + 1^2} = \text{distance}$$
$$\sqrt{9 + 1} = \text{distance}$$
$$\sqrt{10} = \text{distance}$$
$$3.1623 \approx \text{distance}$$